Endangered & Extinct Species

Series Editor: Cara Acred

Volume 260

Independence Educational Publishers

First published by Independence Educational Publishers

The Studio, High Green

Great Shelford

Cambridge CB22 5EG

England

© Independence 2014

British Library Cataloguing in Publication Data

Endangered & extinct species. -- (Issues ; 260)

1. Endangered species. 2. Nature conservation.

3. Biodiversity.

I. Series II. Acred, Cara editor.

578.6'8-dc23

ISBN-13: 9781861686756

Printed in Great Britain

MWL Print Group Ltd

Contents

Introduction

Endangered & Extinct Species is Volume 260 in the **ISSUES** series. The aim of the series is to offer current, diverse information about important issues in our world, from a UK perspective.

ABOUT ENDANGERED & EXTINCT SPECIES

Today, a frightening proportion of mammals, birds, reptiles and plants are in danger of becoming extinct. But why should we care? This book explores the problems faced by endangered and extinct species, both globally and in the UK. It examines their importance and considers issues such as tiger poaching, wildlife trafficking and the demand for ivory. *Endangered & Extinct Species* also looks at wildlife conservation efforts across the world.

OUR SOURCES

Titles in the **ISSUES** series are designed to function as educational resource books, providing a balanced overview of a specific subject.

The information in our books is comprised of facts, articles and opinions from many different sources, including:

⇨ Newspaper reports and opinion pieces

⇨ Website factsheets

⇨ Magazine and journal articles

⇨ Statistics and surveys

⇨ Government reports

⇨ Literature from special interest groups

A NOTE ON CRITICAL EVALUATION

Because the information reprinted here is from a number of different sources, readers should bear in mind the origin of the text and whether the source is likely to have a particular bias when presenting information (or when conducting their research). It is hoped that, as you read about the many aspects of the issues explored in this book, you will critically evaluate the information presented.

It is important that you decide whether you are being presented with facts or opinions. Does the writer give a biased or unbiased report? If an opinion is being expressed, do you agree with the writer? Is there potential bias to the 'facts' or statistics behind an article?

ASSIGNMENTS

In the back of this book, you will find a selection of assignments designed to help you engage with the articles you have been reading and to explore your own opinions. Some tasks will take longer than others and there is a mixture of design, writing and research based activities that you can complete alone or in a group.

FURTHER RESEARCH

At the end of each article we have listed its source and a website that you can visit if you would like to conduct your own research. Please remember to critically evaluate any sources that you consult and consider whether the information you are viewing is accurate and unbiased.

Useful weblinks

www.bats.org.uk

www.careforthewild.com

www.conservation.org

www.discoveringgalapagos.org.uk

www.greenpeace.org

www.ifaw.org

www.nps.gov

www.panthera.org

www.savegalapagos.org

www.theconversation.com

www.ypte.org.uk

www.wildlife.co.uk

www.wwf.org.uk

Endangered animals of the world

A factsheet from Young People's Trust for the Environment.

Endangered means to be under threat or near extinction. When a species/animal is endangered it means that they are disappearing fast or have a very small population – not large enough to survive. Extinction means the end of existence for a species.

The IUCN (International Union for Conservation of Nature) have what is known as a Red List. This red list is a guide to how endangered a species is – animals are measured on a scale from 'Least Concern' to the worst 'Extinct'.

Here's a look at just a few of the world's most endangered species:

Greater Horseshoe Bat

Rhinolophus ferrumequinum

IUCN status: least concern

Population trend: decreasing

There are 18 species of bat in Britain and all of them are endangered. The greater horseshoe bat is one of the rarest. One reason for their decline is the destruction of suitable roosting sites, such as old buildings and hollow trees. Changing land use from woodland and small fields to large scale agriculture has also had an effect. They have also suffered from the use of insecticides (poisonous chemicals sprayed onto crops to kill harmful insects) which have deprived the bats of their insect food. Due to conservation efforts its population in the UK has stabilized at about 5,000.

Siberian (Amur) Tiger

Cold, snowy Siberia, Russia, is home to the largest of all the tigers, the Siberian tiger.

Panthera tigris ssp. altaica

IUCN status: Endangered

Population trend: stable

Population: It is highly endangered although its numbers have increased from an all-time low of 20 in the 1930s. There are now an estimated 360 Amur tigers in the wild, according to the IUCN. Hunting and loss of habitat have reduced their numbers and there is little genetic diversity in the remaining population, increasing their vulnerability There is also a tiny population remaining in China of around 20 individuals.

Loggerhead Turtle

Caretta caretta

IUCN status: Endangered

This threatened reptile lives in the Mediterranean Sea, as well as the Black Sea and Atlantic Ocean. In the past its main dangers were hunting for its shell and meat. Now it has to put up with tourists disturbing the sandy beaches where it lays its eggs. In Turkey, hotels have been built right on its breeding sites. Out at sea, the turtles sometimes become entangled in fishing nets and drown. A possible new threat to them may be the increase in sand temperatures which determines the sex of the turtle. Warmer temperatures could result in an excess of females!

Northern Bald Ibis

Geronticus eremita

IUCN status: Critically endangered

Population trend: decreasing

Population: Morocco is home to 95% of the truly wild colonies of the ibis where populations are increasing and now number over 500 birds. Syria also has a small and declining population with only five mature birds. Parts of North Africa and the Middle East are visited by these migrating birds. Turkey also have a healthy semi-wild population of reintroduced birds, numbering 91 in

2006 (IUCN). However, the use of pesticides on the marshes and grasslands where it lives is reducing the numbers.

Part of the ibis' decline is due to natural causes. It nests high above the ground and its eggs are so round that some of them roll out of the nest and break. However, disturbance of nesting sites and feeding grounds is a more significant factor. The Ancient Egyptians used to depict this bird in their hieroglyphic writing, but it no longer lives in Egypt.

Beginning of life

Life began on our planet about 3,500 million years ago. The first living things were found in the sea, and over the course of millions of years, from these early life forms, a rich variety of animals has descended. Through the process we call evolution, animals have become adapted to enable them to live in all parts of the world, sometimes in the most hostile environments.

Almost 600 million years ago, the invertebrates appeared i.e. those animals without backbones – insects and other minibeasts. The earliest vertebrates i.e. animals with backbones, were in the form of primitive fish and appeared around 500 million years ago. From these, all the other fishes descended, as well as amphibians, reptiles, birds and mammals.

The animal kingdom is enormous and we do not know for certain how many species there are in the world. Around 1.5 million species of animal have been named and described by scientists – and over a million of these are insects. It is known that there are about twice as many animals in tropical rainforests than in any other habitat, and it is here that there are likely to be countless numbers of species yet unknown to science. It has been estimated that the total number of insect species alone could be around 30 million!

It is just possible, but unlikely, that there are a few large animals remaining to be discovered, but what we can be sure of is that the most numerous large animal on Earth is *Homo sapiens* – the human! Modern man appeared about 30,000 years ago and has increasingly come to dominate the planet. The steady increase in population was speeded up by advances in civilization such as the Industrial Revolution and better health and medical care.

The rate in increase of the human population is slowing down in parts of the Northern Hemisphere, but it continues to rise in Third World countries, despite the effect of famine, floods, disease and war. Allowing for the death rate, over one million more humans come into the world each week!

This population explosion means that millions of people suffer from hunger and disease, and more and more wild places are taken over, causing animals and plants to suffer too.

Extinction is for ever!

As almost everyone knows, to become extinct is to be gone forever. Even before human's arrival on Earth, species became extinct quite naturally. Natural extinction happens when a species declines in numbers gradually but steadily at the end of its evolutionary period on Earth. The length of this period depends on how well a species can adapt to changes in climate and changes in other animals and plants around it. This process of extinction can take a very long time – sometimes several million years – and the extinction of one species is immediately followed by the appearance of another in a continuous cycle.

The case of the dinosaurs is the most well-known example of natural extinction. These reptiles appeared on Earth about 200 million years ago and dominated both land and sea for almost 100 million years. It is not certain why the dinosaurs became extinct, but their disappearance was a natural one and new species of animals evolved to replace them.

The rate of extinction has speeded up unnaturally over the last 400 years, rising sharply since 1900. This increase in the rate of extinction is directly related to the increase in the human population over the same period of time. The vast number of humans has caused great damage to the planet, as wild habitats have been taken over, forcing animals and plants into smaller and smaller areas, until some of them have become extinct. We have also polluted some habitats with chemicals and refuse, making them unfit for wildlife. These causes of extinction are known as indirect destruction.

Animals may also become extinct through direct destruction. This includes the hunting and

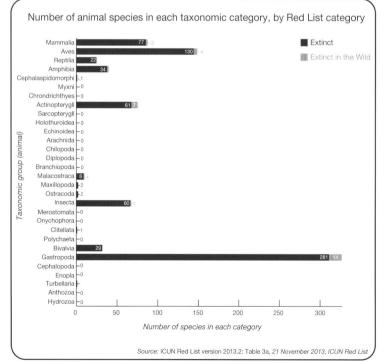

Number of animal species in each taxonomic category, by Red List category

Taxonomic group (animal)

■ Extinct
■ Extinct in the Wild

Mammalia	77
Aves	130
Reptilia	22
Amphibia	34
Cephalaspidomorphi	1
Myxni	0
Chrondrichthyes	0
Actinopterygll	61
Sarcopterygll	0
Holothuroidea	0
Echinoidea	0
Arachnida	0
Chilopoda	0
Diplopoda	0
Branchiopoda	0
Malacostraca	8
Maxillopoda	2
Ostracoda	2
Insecta	60
Merostomata	0
Onychophora	0
Clitellata	1
Polychaeta	0
Bivalvia	29
Gastropoda	281
Cephalopoda	0
Enopla	0
Turbellaria	
Anthozoa	0
Hydrozoa	0

Number of species in each category

Source: ICUN Red List version 2013.2: Table 3a, 21 November 2013, ICUN Red List

capturing of animals. Humans have always hunted and killed wildlife but early humans lived more in harmony with nature, they killed animals for essentials like food and clothing. When guns were invented mass destruction of species was possible. Animals have been, and still are, killed for meat, clothing, medicines, feathers, eggs, trophies, tourist souvenirs – and sometimes just for amusement. Some species are still captured in the wild for the live pet trade, even though their numbers are dwindling.

The extinction of at least 500 species of animals has been caused by man, most of them in this century. Today there are about 5,000 endangered animals and at least one species dies out every year. There are probably many more which become extinct without anyone knowing.

The main threats to species then can be cited as poaching, habitat loss and climate change. The International Union for Conservation of Nature has its own 'red list' of endangered species ranging from 'least concern' through to 'critically endangered'. It is their assessment which we'll refer to here.

The dodo has become a symbol of extinction. It was a turkey-sized flightless pigeon which lived on the island of Mauritius. When sailors landed on the island for the first time in the sixteenth century, they killed the helpless bird for food. The dodo's eggs and young were eaten by dogs, cats, pigs, rats and monkeys which man had introduced to the island. The dodo, unused to predators, very quickly declined in numbers – and it was extinct by 1681.

Is it Important to save animals from extinction?

Some people may ask 'why bother with conservation?' We now realise that it is important to maintain the planet's biodiversity, that it is the richness (variety) of animal and plant life, its abundance and wild habitats. The more species disappear, the more entire eco-systems become vulnerable and would eventually fall apart as the links in the food chains become broken. For example certain animals only eat certain plants and those plants may need that animal to pollinate it or spread its seed. Without one, the other is also likely to die out.

From a selfish point of view, we humans never know how valuable a species of animal or plant may be for us in the future, perhaps as food, medicines (particularly plants) or specific information.

Saving endangered animals

People all over the world are working to help save endangered animals from extinction. There are conservation organisations which try to make people aware of the problems facing wild animals. Some of the ways in which they are being saved include habitat protection, captive breeding, setting up nature reserves

and parks and using alternative products in place of products from rare animals.

Governments can help by making international agreements between countries to protects animals (many countries, for example, have agreed to stop hunting the blue whale) and their habitats. There has been agreement from a number of countries in June 2010 to protect the rainforests and prevent deforestation through financial backing.

Scientists are setting up gene banks in which they keep an animal's genetic material (the 'building blocks' of a living thing) in suspended animation. This technique may make it possible in the future to 'grow' a new animal of the same species. Kew Gardens, London has a seed bank in case plant species become extinct in the wild.

You can help too!

The first step towards saving animals is to learn as much as possible about them. If we know where and how they live, and what they need to survive, then it will be easier to help them. It is also a good idea to learn from our mistakes of the past, such as destroying too much rainforest and over-hunting animals. To ensure the survival of the world's animals we must learn how to keep 'sustainable populations' alive i.e. populations with enough numbers for the animals to survive on their own. The dodo and all the other which man has made extinct became so because their populations fell below a sustainable level. It is worth keeping in mind that those animals may well become the endangered animals of tomorrow.

⇨ The above information is reprinted with kind permission from the Young People's Trust for the Environment. Please visit www.ypte.org.uk for further information.

Extinction: just how bad is it and why should we care?

An article from The Conversation.

By Euan Ritchie, Senior Lecturer in Ecology at Deakin University

'Dad, the world is missing amazing animals. I wish extinction wasn't forever.'

Despite my wife and I working as biologists, our five-year-old son came to make this statement independently.

He is highlighting what I and many others consider to be society's biggest challenge, and arguably failure: the continuing loss of species from Earth. The massive impact we are having on the planet has firmly entrenched us in a period of our history commonly called the Anthropocene.

The environment was front and centre of public consciousness and a key election focus in Australia in 2007, but following the global financial crisis and continuing economic uncertainty, we seem to care less and less about the environment and more and more about budgets and surpluses.

If the environment were a bank and species its money, it would need a rescue package that would make the recent European bail-outs look insignificant.

The state of extinction

We still have little idea of how many species exist on Earth. Only a fraction (~1.5 million of an estimated five million) have been formally described, and even fewer assessed for their conservation status. How do we conserve what we don't know exists?

If Earth were a house, it would be as though we had listed the contents of only one room, and even then were not aware of their true value, while simultaneously the house was being demolished.

It is important to note that extinction – the permanent loss of species – is a natural process that is counterpoint to speciation, the creation of new species through evolution.

Background or 'normal' rates of extinction vary through time but are typically in the order of one to two species per year. Current rates of extinction, however, are estimated to have reached 1,000 to 10,000 times this rate. Put bluntly, the annual species body count is no longer a mere handful, it's an avalanche.

There have been at least five episodes of mass extinctions in the past, during which anywhere from 60 to 96% of existing species became extinct. Indeed, 99% of all existing species that have ever existed are now extinct.

Volcanic eruptions and asteroid impacts are among the prime suspects as the cause of previous mass extinctions – including the oft-cited demise of the dinosaurs. Yes, extinctions, even mass extinctions, are not unprecedented. The difference this time is that humanity is the cause of the Earth's sixth mass extinction event, through such anthropogenic impacts as habitat loss and modification, the spread of invasive species, and climate change.

Farewelling species

Some 875 species have been recorded as declining to extinction between 1500 and 2009 which, the observant will note, is entirely consistent with a background of extinction rate of one to two species per year. What, then, are the grounds for supposing that the current rate of extinction actually exceeds this value by such a huge margin?

The key phrase is 'have been recorded'. As already discussed, the majority of species have not been identified or described. A reasonable supposition is that unrecognised species are lost at a rate comparable with that of known ones.

We now also have reasonable estimates of species diversity in particular habitats, such as insects in tropical forests. Our measures of the proportion of such habitats that have been destroyed therefore provide a good basis for estimating species loss. If these estimates are right, we are now living through a period where the rate of extinction is 1,000 to 10,000 times the background rate.

Delving deeper, the *IUCN Red List of Threatened Species* notes that 36% of the 47,677 species assessed are threatened with extinction, which represents 21% of mammals, 30% of amphibians, 12% of birds, 28% of reptiles, 37% of freshwater fishes, 70% of plants and 35% of invertebrates.

More recently we have bid farewell to species such as the Baiji Dolphin, the Alaotra Grebe and the Japanese River Otter. And who could forget the passing of 'Lonesome George', the last individual Pinta Island Tortoise, who died on 24 June 2012? Closer to home, our most recent casualty was a small bat, the Christmas Island Pipistrelle.

There is one brighter note: a recent study by Fisher and Blomberg has shown that depending on species' characteristics and other factors such as the places where they occur, remnant populations of some species may still turn up.

But an exclusive focus on extinction is inappropriate anyway, given that many surviving species are hanging on only by the barest of threads. The dire situation of Australia's marsupials is stark evidence of this. Even iconic and once abundant species such as the Tasmanian Devil are now on the brink of oblivion.

Deep in debt

A further sobering thought is encompassed in the concept of

'extinction debt'. Recent studies in Europe have demonstrated that the species currently at highest risk of extinction most likely got that way because of human actions 50 to 100 years ago.

I'm sure many of us have driven on an Australian country road, admiring the grand old eucalypts that stand alone in the nearby paddocks – remnants of the pre-agricultural landscape. But you may also have noticed that under the big trees there are often no little trees. Hence, when the big trees die, as they inevitably will, there will be nothing to replace them.

If we want to avert extinctions from our legacies we will need to direct conservation efforts most into areas carrying the highest debts.

At our own peril

But why should it matter to us if we have a few less species? The simple answer is that we are connected to and deeply dependent on other species. From pollination of our crops by bees, to carbon storage by our forests, and even the bacteria in our mouths, we rely upon biodiversity for our very existence. We neglect this at our own peril. And of course there are equally justified arguments for keeping species based purely on their aesthetic and cultural importance, or for their own sake.

Doom-and-gloom predictions tend to paralyse us, rather than jolting us into action. So what can be done? There are wonderful examples of individuals and organisations working at both small and large scales to tackle and even sometimes turn back the tide of extinctions.

There are also some compelling personal approaches, such as that of Alejandro Frid who is writing a series of letters to his daughter as a way of confronting the issues of climate change and biodiversity loss. But what is urgently needed, of course, is radical change in society as a whole in the way it interacts with its environment.

Until then, my fellow ecologists and I must continue to work hard to sell our message and spread awareness of society's biggest challenge.

1 May 2013

⇨ The above information is reprinted with kind permission from The Conversation Trust (UK). Please visit www. theconversation.com for further information.

The world's top predators are in decline, and it's hurting us too

An article from The Conversation.

By Euan Ritchie, Senior Lecturer in Ecology at Deakin University

Humans have an innate fear of large predators, and with good reason. Nobody wants to be a shark or lion's next meal.

But new research in the journal *Science* shows that our inability to live with these animals is putting their survival in great danger, and doing untold damage to the environment.

Through modifying the habitats of large predators or killing predators more directly. we are greatly compromising the ecosystems that they help to keep in balance – free of charge. In turn this environmental degradation creates many problems that have severe consequences for humans.

Top dogs (and cats) under threat

For the first time, a team of researchers from the United States, Australia, Italy and Sweden, and led by Professor Bill Ripple at Oregon State University, have analysed the effects of threats such as habitat loss, human persecution and reduced prey on the world's 31 largest mammalian carnivores.

The species studied include lions, tigers, African wild dogs, leopards, cheetahs, wolves, lynx, otters, bears, hyenas and dingoes. Together they span all continents except Antarctica.

Alarmingly, more than three quarters of the 31 large carnivores are in decline, and 17 species occupy less than half of their historical distributions. The Red Wolf in the southeastern United States is now found in less than 1% of its historical range, and the Ethiopian Wolf in just 2%.

Hotspots of carnivore decline are southeast Asia, southern and East Africa, and the Amazon, where several large carnivores are declining. And in the developed world there are now few places where large carnivores remain.

Aside from the intrinsic tragedy of losing any species, what should perhaps concern us even more is that we are only just beginning to understand and appreciate just how important large predators are to maintaining healthy ecosystems, and our dependence on the ecosystem services they deliver.

Ripple effect

Seven carnivore species in particular have been shown to have profound effects on the environment and cause what is known as 'trophic cascades'. A trophic cascade is a ripple effect, where one species' influence spreads through multiple levels of a food web.

Species for which this effect is most well-known are African lions, leopards, Eurasian lynx, cougars, grey wolves, sea otters and dingoes.

In Australia dingoes greatly reduce kangaroo and red fox numbers, which in turn reduces grazing of vegetation and predation of native animals, helping to conserve and protect biodiversity.

In coastal North America, sea otters keep sea urchin numbers in check, which helps maintain kelp forests and benefits other marine species dependent on this habitat. But in this case otters might also offer a defence against climate change, as healthy kelp forests can grow rapidly and store large amounts of carbon.

And in Africa, a decrease in lions and leopards has coincided with a dramatic increase in olive baboons, which threaten farm crops and livestock, and spread intestinal worms. Baboons even impact education, as children have to stay home to defend their farms from raids.

Clearly predators have far-reaching ecological, economic and social benefits that are grossly underappreciated. There is no doubt predators pose challenges too, such as wolves attacking livestock. But education and new management practices offer ways forward. For instance, we could use guardian animals to protect livestock from predators.

Together we call on governments to end policies and management practices that are responsible for the ongoing persecution and loss of predators from our planet. Western Australia's new shark plan is an example of management that fails to account for the science of big predators. Instead we need an international initiative that aims to conserve large predators and promote their coexistence with people.

9 January 2014

⇨ The above information is reprinted with kind permission from The Conversation Trust (UK). Please visit www.theconversation.com for further information.

One of Britain's rarest mammals needs protection

New research shows just 1,000 grey long-eared bats remain in the UK and numbers are declining.

The UK's grey long-eared bats need greater conservation efforts before we lose them' – Dr Orly Razgour is calling for this little-known species to be afforded 'Priority Species' status in the newly published *Conserving grey long-eared bats in our landscape: conservation management plan*.

Dr Razgour is the lead author of the plan. It's based on new research she conducted into the species at the University of Bristol, in collaboration with the Bat Conservation Trust. Her research has shown the estimated population of these bats in the UK is around 1,000 animals and the population is declining. Prior to her study it had been hoped the bats were more numerous, sadly her findings confirm how very rare they are.

The bats are confined to small pockets along the south coast of England, including the Isle of Wight, with a small number found in the Channel Islands and a single record from South Wales.

The UK grey long-eared bat population comprises two distinct genetic groups and Dr Razgour is concerned that the low numbers mean the future survival of the species in the UK is questionable, unless more is done to protect the remaining few. She calls for more work to identify, monitor and protect maternity roost sites, where female bats raise their young, and hibernation sites.

Dr Orly Razgour

'Despite being one the rarest UK mammals, up until recently there was very little known about the grey long-eared bat and what it needs to survive. Studying the grey long-eared bat, I realised that the plight of this bat demonstrates many of the threats and conservation challenges facing wildlife, from the effects of habitat loss and climate change to the problem of small isolated populations.

The UK grey long-eared bat population has been declining and has become fragmented in the past century. This decline and fragmentation is likely to be in response to the dramatic decline of lowland meadows and marshlands, the bat's main foraging habitats. The long-term survival of the grey long-eared bat UK population is closely linked to the conservation of these lowland meadows and marshland habitats. The conservation management plan is calling to prioritise the conservation status of the grey long-eared bat and use this bat as a flagship species to promote the conservation and restoration of lowland grasslands.'

Habitat destroyed

Lowland meadows and marshland habitats have all but disappeared in the UK following changes to land management and farming practices in the latter half of the last century. As these bats prey on agricultural pests, encouraging these bats in the farmed landscape may benefit the wider farming community if bat numbers increase dramatically.

Traditionally a cave-dwelling species, grey long-eared bats have become dependent on our buildings for roost sites. Their roost requirements are specific; they need large open spaces in lofts and barns close to foraging habitat. These roosts are under threat from building development and Dr Razgour is calling for identification, monitoring and protection of roost sites and their surrounding grassland area.

Key findings of Dr Razgour's research

The grey long-eared bat should be afforded 'Priority Species' status by Natural England and the Department for Environment, Food and Rural Affairs to ensure that more funds are directed towards protecting its habitat.

Maternity roosts and hibernation sites need to be identified, monitored and protected.

The landscape around and between roosts needs to be protected to increase grassland foraging habitat

Notes for editors

Dr Orly Razgour is the lead author of the report and undertook the research during her PhD at the University of Bristol, which was funded by the Hon. Vincent Weir and was carried out in collaboration with the Bat Conservation Trust. The management plan was written as a collaborative project between the Bat Conservation Trust, the University of Bristol and ecological consultants who have worked with the species (Daniel Whitby and Erika Dahlberg).

The Bat Conservation Trust (BCT) is the only national organisation solely devoted to the conservation of bats and their habitats in the UK. Its network of 100 local bat groups and more than 1,000 bat workers survey roosts and hibernation sites, and work with householders, builders, farmers and foresters to protect bats.

The National Bat Helpline 0845 1300 228 is for anyone who finds a grounded or injured bat, believes bats to be at risk and for anyone who thinks they may have bats in their building or wants to let us know about a bat roost site.

5 August 2013

⇨ The above information is reprinted with kind permission from the Bat Conservation Trust. Please visit www.bats.org.uk for further information.

Prince William speaks about his feelings towards endangered animals after the birth of his son

The Duke of Cambridge has spoken movingly about how the birth of his son has increased the depth of his feelings towards endangered animals.

William was left close to tears after being shown footage of a rhino attacked by poachers and left bleeding to death during filming for a TV documentary.

The royal was interviewed in July soon after the birth of his son Prince George and in the programme, screened by ITV and CNN, talks about his passion for wildlife and how fatherhood has changed him.

But it's not just nature's impressive big animals that have an effect on the royal, he also revealed how he is 'not so good' with spiders and snakes.

Documentary film maker Jane Treays, writing in the latest edition of the *Radio Times*, described the build up to the interview for the ITV programme and the events on the day.

During the informal chat filmed at Kensington Palace, William, who has a strong interest in animal conservation, told her: 'The wildlife is incredibly vulnerable and I feel a real protective instinct, more so now that I am a father, which is why I get emotional about it... you want to stand up for what is very vulnerable and needs protecting.

'Elephants, rhinos and many other animals that are persecuted don't have a voice.'

Ms Treays wrote that William became emotional when shown footage of the rhino, 'watching pictures of a butchered rhino bleeding to death. Tears well in his eyes and he confesses to everything being changed by the birth of his son.'

The Duke says in the documentary: 'It's just so powerful. You'd think something that big and that's been around so long, would have worked out a way to avoid being caught and persecuted, but they really don't. I do feel anger, but I also feel really great hope that we will overcome this as a human race.'

William's family, from his grandfather the Duke of Edinburgh to his mother Diana, Princess of Wales, have inspired him to champion causes he believes in.

The Duke said: 'The legacy is quite a daunting one, following on from my grandfather and father. It just sort of happened... My mother would come back with all these stories, full of excitement and passion for what she had been doing and I used to sit there, quite a surprised little boy, taking it all in – and the infectious enthusiasm and energy she had rubbed off on me.'

William's interest in Africa's natural world is reflected in his royal patronage of the UK-based African wildlife conservation charity Tusk Trust.

The Cambridges will attend the organisation's inaugural awards ceremony in central London on Thursday night.

Two awards will be presented, a lifetime achievement honour named after the duke and another recognising an up-and-coming conservationist, with the ceremony filmed for the documentary.

In the programme, William stressed his love of the continent: 'Africa, emotionally and mentally, has affected me. It's magical. Every time I go back it brings out new things. This is a lifelong commitment and I'll always be involved... no matter what.'

Africa is also a place where he can be himself, he told Ms Treays: 'I love the fact you can go into any village in Kenya or the east coast of Africa and just walk in and have a chat with someone and they have absolutely no idea who you are. Usually my Swahili stops after about two sentences but we muddle through in English.'

He revealed that he uses the continent's wildlife to help stay relaxed: 'I've got hundreds of animals on my iPhone, noises and sounds of the bush, so if I'm having a stressful day, I'll put a buffalo, a cricket or a newt on and it takes you back instantly to the bush. And it does completely settle me down.'

Speaking about endangered animals the duke said: 'It's horrifying. It's hard to put into words, the depth of sadness that I would feel if they became extinct.'

He added: 'I want the (Tusk Trust) awards to be credible in the conservation world and for those who receive them to realise how fantastic their work has been. They are leading the way. Now is the time to galvanise and energise all the people who want to help.'

Tusk Trust establishes and promotes community-driven conservation programmes in Africa and William told Ms Treays he realised it had to work with local people whose livelihood could be threatened by wild animals.

He said: 'We have to remember how desperately poor these guys are... this is all they have known, living in these communities with their cattle and goats, and they will protect them to their last breath. Their water and grazing is in very short supply. Conservation has to have these communities' blessing.'

But he stressed education was a major weapon in fighting illegal poaching: 'The way they are doing things is getting more and more sophisticated. As soon as you find a way of dealing with it, they find another.

'Education is such a huge, important issue, to educate everyone involved in the illegal markets about the damage that can be done and the implications of what they are doing.'

Asked by Ms Treays about the legacy for Prince George he laughed: 'At the moment, the only legacy I want to pass on to him is to sleep more and maybe not to have to change his nappy quite so many times, but as he gets older I'm sure he'll pick up the bug of conservation.'

10 September 2013

⇨ The above information is reprinted with kind permission from the Press Association. Please visit www.pressassociation.com for further information.

Reducing ivory and rhino horn demand is key to the species' survival

Legal trade and military-style protection may help, but ultimately elephants and rhinos will not survive with their ecological function intact unless demand and price falls.

By Adam Welz

Astonishing numbers of elephants and rhinos are being poached across Africa. Between 25,000 and 40,000 elephants are likely to be illegally killed there this year. South Africa, home to about 80% of the continent's rhinoceroses, is projected to lose between 900 and 1,000 of those primeval beasts to poachers by Christmas, up from a mere 13 in 2007.

Governments and conservation organisations are struggling to contain the rising carnage, a result of increasing demand for rhino horn and ivory in Asia, especially in China, Vietnam and Thailand.

I recently wrote about some proposed solutions to the problem for two US-based environmental magazines, *Ensia* and *Yale e360*. Although I've followed the poaching issue for years, researching these articles has heightened my sense of it being, to use an appropriate metaphor, a 'blind-men-and-an-elephant' problem.

Stopping the onslaught of poachers is a daunting, complicated task. It requires understanding the economics of the illegal wildlife trade, the methods of the criminals engaging in it, the psychology of those buying its products and the biology of the animals being killed.

Many experts that I've interviewed understand only part of the problem and the solutions they propose are strongly coloured by personal expertise. Unsurprisingly, economists often put forward market-based solutions, legislators push more laws, police want better law enforcement, soldiers say they need more drones and guns, politicians think more speeches and treaties are useful, and conservationists with no deep experience in any of these fields tend to favour whichever solutions they're most exposed to.

Most of those trying to save elephants and rhinos are intensely emotionally invested in their struggle. I can relate to them, because every time I encounter wild elephants I'm amazed by their power, their intelligence and their sense of fun. Rhinos are perhaps the nearest living thing we have to dinosaurs. The thought of the next generation not being able to experience these pachyderms is heartbreaking. We've recently lost the Western black rhino and the Vietnamese subspecies of Javan rhino to poachers, so the fear of further extinctions is not at all irrational.

But this desperate emotional investment combined with many individuals' limited exposure to aspects of the poaching problem has led, in my opinion, to an unhelpful amount of conflict among conservationists and the decision-makers whose actions will decide the future of elephants and rhinos.

Opposing views have become strongly entrenched, and instead of acknowledging that there can be disagreement among honest people about the solutions to wildlife crime, many activists are quick to demonise those with differing ideas. Instead of asking more questions and together exploring the possible implications of various courses of action (because no one can, in my opinion, cover enough mental ground to take it all in alone) many pay lip service to the complexity of the issue and refuse to engage

meaningfully with the 'opposition' who, as it happens, want to save elephants and rhinos just as much as they do.

One extremely divisive potential solution that I explore in my *Ensia* article is to re-legalise the international trade in rhino horn, which has been largely banned since 1976. South African state and private stockpiles contain over 18 tonnes of horn recovered from dead animals and de-horning operations, which could be worth hundreds of millions of dollars if it were allowed to be sold at today's black market prices. The only people currently making money from the rhino horn trade are criminals, and it's extraordinarily frustrating to some rhino custodians that they could fund conservation by selling these stockpiles if they were allowed to sell them.

Another potential solution is to adopt military equipment and tactics in the fight against poachers. This is the first-used option of many wildlife managers, and understandably so. Poachers don't drop in with jasmine garlands in their hair to politely present you with tea and a plate of home-

baked cookies; they're often blooded, hard men with military training and increasingly sophisticated weapons who are a threat not just to animals but to people. I'd want my own squad of hard men with guns if I managed a wildlife reserve.

Military-style solutions to poaching are popular because there are many examples that when looked at in isolation seem to confirm their success, albeit success that comes at a high price in dollars and human lives. (Military-grade equipment costs millions, and poachers and game rangers are regularly killed in firefights.)

For example, when I visited the Ol Pejeta Conservancy in Kenya in late 2011, they'd lost five of their famous rhinos that year to poachers. In response, they'd recently employed a just-retired British soldier to train a new anti-poaching squad equipped with Heckler and Koch assault rifles. Ol Pejeta lost no rhinos to poachers in 2012, and has lost only one so far this year.

But poaching in Kenya as a whole has gone up since 2011. The rhino and elephant slaughterers may be

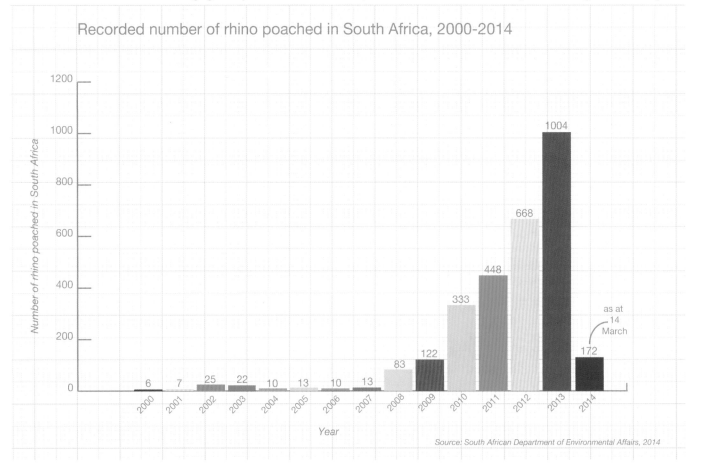

Recorded number of rhino poached in South Africa, 2000-2014

Source: South African Department of Environmental Affairs, 2014

avoiding Ol Pejeta, but they're hitting less well-protected areas of the country. As I explain in my *Yale e360* article, researchers of the illegal drug trade call this the 'balloon effect'. If you push down drug production in one area – for example by destroying coca crops in one part of Colombia – it pops up elsewhere. It's simply proved impossible to control illegal activity across large, remote areas when a lucrative market for that activity's products – e.g. cocaine – persists. Despite the US having spent billions on enforcement and interdiction operations in Latin America as part of the 'war on drugs', drug production remains high and murderous drug smuggling gangs remain extremely powerful. As many observers point out, the same criminals who smuggle drugs also often smuggle illegal wildlife products.

Some people have already started breeding rhino and regularly harvesting their horns in anticipation of legal trade. (The horn contains no nerves, so cutting it off is painless, and it grows back over a few years. No equivalent procedure is practical for elephants.) Their idea is to ensure the future of rhinos by create a profitable business supplying horn over the long term, which would pay for their expensive security and incentivise more people to breed them.

This might work. If legal horn farming turns out to be profitable, we might end up with many more rhinos than we have today. I'm concerned about what sort of rhinos those will be, though, because the most economical way to keep them for horn harvesting purposes is in dense concentrations, a bit like cattle in paddocks, where it's cheaper to manage and guard them compared to when they're free-ranging in large, wild areas.

Initiating a legal trade in rhino horn or ivory will not automatically remove the incentive to poach rhinos and elephants. A black market in these commodities is likely to persist if retail prices remain high, and there is no shortage of poor people in Africa who will risk their lives for the prospect of earning a life-changing amount of cash by shooting one animal, especially when the chances of being caught are low. This means

that even those rhino custodians who aren't involved in the horn trade and who aren't managing their animals for maximum profit may be forced to confine their rhinos to small 'intensive protection zones', because it's near-impossible to protect wide-ranging animals across massive, rugged areas like the large national parks and wilderness areas of Africa.

If the only practical way that we can protect animals is to confine them to small areas, the only sorts of rhinos and elephants we'll have will be ecologically useless ones. They'll look like the beasts we know, but they'll no longer be able to fulfil their vital roles in the forests, savannas and drylands. Africa will have 'paper pachyderms' to complement its many 'paper parks', those national parks which exist on maps but serve no real conservation purpose because they're not managed and have been destroyed by settlers, miners and hunters.

Rhinos and elephants are ecosystem engineers, which means that Africa's iconic ecosystems look and work the way they do because these animals have helped shape them over millions of years. Elephants and black rhinos maintain savannas by knocking down trees and munching bushes. White rhinos create 'grazing lawns' for other herbivores to feed on. Elephants spread the seeds of forest trees and dig waterholes in dry river beds that countless other animals rely on to get through the dry season. All megaherbivores transport vital nutrients through landscapes. If wide-ranging elephants and rhinos are removed from Africa, its ecosystems will change fundamentally.

I'm not sure how large numbers of ecologically functional rhinos and elephants will survive unless the demand for and the price that users are prepared to pay for their products comes down drastically, which is why I've come to believe that persuading people not to buy rhino horn and new ivory, so-called 'demand reduction', is ultimately the most relevant part of the multi-faceted struggle to save these magnificent animals and the grand, diverse ecosystems that they're part of. YouTube movies, social media campaigns and thousands of people talking to their friends might not be as

sexy as machine gun-toting, drone-flying anti-poaching armies, but I think they're worth far more investment and attention than they're currently receiving.

I know that by saying this I'm opening myself up to attack. I've already been accused of being seduced by an organisation called WildAid that believes strongly in demand reduction and been lambasted on social media for writing about legal trade, which, apparently, is so wrong an idea that it shouldn't even be mentioned in public. I've also been told that writers like me shouldn't have opinions on the things they write about, even though I try to be clear about when I'm reporting as neutrally as possible on issues and when I'm delivering opinions on them.

If you, dear reader, are inclined to join the mud-slinging parade, please consider the following: I'm open to the possibility that my view of the potential and importance of demand reduction is because I'm a biased 'blind man' who has spent a large chunk of his life working in the media, and none in law enforcement, the military or commerce. I might not have understood significant parts of the poaching problem, so I'm not claiming to have the answer. I'm not even advocating the removal of emotion from the debate.

What I am saying is that I'm not sure how large, ecologically functional populations of rhinos and elephants will survive across their historic ranges in Africa (and Asia) if the price of and demand for newly harvested rhino horn and ivory remain high. I remain curious about solutions to the poaching problem and am open to changing my mind in the face of new information and argument. I hope you are, too.

28 August 2013

⇨ The above information is reprinted with kind permission from *The Guardian*. Please visit www.theguardian.com for further information.

Licence to kill

How deforestation for palm oil is driving Sumatran tigers towards extinction.

Executive summary

As few as 400 tigers are thought to remain in the rainforests of Sumatra, which are vanishing at a staggering rate – a quarter of a million hectares every year. Expansion of oil palm and pulpwood plantations was responsible for nearly two-thirds of the destruction of tiger habitat from 2009 to 2011, the most recent period for which official Indonesian Government data are available. Such destruction fragments the extensive tracts of rainforest over which tigers need to range in order to hunt. It also increases their contact with humans; this leads to more poaching for tiger skins and traditional medicines and more tiger attacks, resulting in both tiger and human deaths.

'I do not want to explain to my granddaughter Almira that we, in our time, could not save the forests and the people that depend on it.'

President Susilo Bambang Yudhoyono, 27 September 2011

The decline of Sumatran tigers is a measure of the loss of rainforest, biodiversity and also climate stability. This summer huge fires, both accidental and deliberate, raged across the Sumatran province of Riau, destroying hundreds of thousands of hectares of rainforests – including the deep peatland forests that are a last stand of tiger habitat in the province. The fires released record amounts of greenhouse gas (GHG) emissions and pollutants in a haze that stretched as far as Thailand.

According to the Indonesian Government, 85% of the country's GHG emissions typically come from land-use changes (principally related to deforestation for plantations or agriculture), and around half of this is peat-related. Even Sumatran tiger habitat in protected areas such as the world-famous Tesso Nilo National Park has been virtually destroyed by encroachment for illegal palm oil production, and government officials acknowledge that protection for such areas exists only on paper.

Forested tiger habitat in licensed plantation concessions has no protection at all. One million hectares – 10% of all remaining forested tiger habitat – remained at risk of clearance in pulp and oil palm concessions in 2011. Over the 2009–2011 period, the APRIL pulp and paper group was responsible for a sixth of the deforestation of tiger habitat. Over the same period, the palm oil sector cleared a quarter of the tiger habitat remaining in its concessions.

These failures expose how unregulated and irresponsible expansion, notably of oil palm and pulpwood plantations, undermines the Indonesian Government's commitments to stop deforestation and to save the tiger and other endangered wildlife.

Greenpeace's investigations have revealed that household names including Colgate-Palmolive, Mondelez International (formerly Kraft), Neste Oil, Procter & Gamble, Reckitt Benckiser and a host of other companies are linked to Singapore-based Wilmar International Ltd and its international trade in dirty palm oil. Wilmar is the world's largest palm oil processor, accounting for over one-third of the global palm oil processing market and with a distribution network covering over 50 countries.

Although Wilmar has undertaken to preserve high conservation value (HCV) forests and peatland on its own concessions, these areas supply less than 4% of the palm oil it trades and refines, with the remainder being produced by third-party suppliers. In relation to Wilmar, Greenpeace has documented deep peatland fires in oil palm concessions; wholesale rainforest destruction and illegal oil palm plantations within the Tesso Nilo National Park, harvests from which have previously been tracked to Wilmar's own mills and which continue to feed into Indonesia's palm oil supply chain; and extensive clearance of both tiger and orangutan habitat. Wilmar is known to own, have a significant stake in or trade with most of the producers Greenpeace has documented as engaging in such irresponsible or illegal activities.

Palm oil has many uses and many benefits, and Greenpeace recognises this; but palm oil production can also have unjustifiable costs. In Indonesia, the costs of irresponsible, unregulated palm oil production include the destruction of the rainforests and peatlands that are the life-blood of endangered species such as the Sumatran tiger and the orangutan.

Greenpeace believes that Wilmar and the household brands that buy its palm oil must recognise the true costs of irresponsible palm oil production. They need to ensure that their palm oil supply makes a genuine contribution to Indonesia's development, rather than destroying the future for its people, its wildlife and the global climate on which we all depend.

22 October 2013

⇨ The above information is reprinted with kind permission from Greenpeace International. Please visit www.greenpeace.org for further information.

Confessions of a tiger poacher

Jose Louies, Head of Enforcement for the Wildlife Trust of India (WTI), reveals the amazing story of how six notorious tiger poachers were caught and convicted in a joint operation with BTR Tiger Reserve, thanks to funding by Care for the Wild's supporters.

Part one

'Another ten minutes' says tiger hunter Dale Singh, as he accompanies our Care for the Wild informer network team in India. We are inside the Biligiriranga Swamy Temple wildlife sanctuary and Dale is leading us to his tiger traps. We must remove them before they are activated by a tiger or leopard. Unfortunately, this also means we are quite literally, walking into the tiger's den.

Despite the area being well known for its tigers, leopards and elephants, it is shocking to think that poaching activities are taking place almost undetected so close to towns and villages. Unfortunately we have had to step up our efforts to meet the increasing demand seen throughout India. Dale's four-member poaching gang was detained by the forest department just a few hours earlier so we are wasting no time bringing him back to the site in the hope of saving tigers from the jaws of his traps.

In disguise

The poachers are just a handful of traditional tiger hunters whose work feeds the illegal tiger trade throughout India and beyond. They move around disguised as street vendors, setting up camps near tiger reserves. The group identify prime tiger habitats using their excellent tracking skills and set up their deadly traps, often waiting just a few days inside the forest for their prize. Once a tiger is trapped, the poachers will kill it and remove the skin. The body is buried within the forest so the bones can be recovered safely a few days later.

Dale leads us to a dry riverbed and after scanning the bank points out two large boulders which formed the basis of their camp. There are no immediate signs of a camp and the area could easily have been overlooked by rangers on patrol. It is only as we draw closer that the remains of a fire and some rubbish suggest that anyone had been there. Sitting on the ground, Dale removes some dry leaves covering an opening beneath one of the boulders and pulls out cooking utensils and food. We decide the abandoned camp is a good place for a break as we have been walking in the heat for some hours. I am amazed at how calm he is and try to get him to open up about his dangerous and illegal occupation, hoping it will help our team understand how poachers think.

'It is just bad luck we were caught, otherwise we would have been back and collected what we came for', he smiles as he smokes a cigarette. His statement is matter of fact and I realised that this is someone who is used to securing their prize. Dale tells me he is part of the Bawaria tribe from Kalka, Haryana. He has trapped a few animals in the past in Assam, Madhya Pradesh and Rajasthan. This is his first trip poaching in southern India and he has never been caught in the past with an animal article in his possession.

Part two

The investigators found out that this was Dale Singh's first trip to South India and he had never been caught by the authorities with an animal article in his possession to date.

'I was almost caught once but managed to escape. A policeman had once apprehended me at a railway station and questioned me for quite some time but couldn't get any information out of me! They searched my belongings in vain trying to find something suspicious but of course nothing turned up. They never even bothered to check the bundles which were in the hands of the children with me. Now had they looked in there, there would have been enough "evidence" to put me away for a long, long time,' Dale Singh said to me.

'Kalka Mata's (a mythical Hindu goddess who rides a tiger) blessings were there with me that day. Without the goddess's hand on our head we would have never walked off unscathed.'

Our team learnt more from Dale Singh about his accomplices. Another poacher arrested alongside him was described as a 'regular' and had previously been arrested but escaped conviction. His wife, financed by a middleman, posted his bail and a few days later he was back with the poaching gang and was on the run from authorities.

A couple of weeks passed and the financier came to visit his family. Now he was trapped in a cycle of poaching, told to gather tiger skins and given logistical support to do so until the loaned bail money was repaid. 'He agreed to it. Why wouldn't he? He was in dire need of money anyway. None of us manage to make enough with the scrap deals that we strike for a living.'

The financier gave each of the gang 3,000–4,000 rupees (£30–40) for expenses, four new vicious looking leg-traps used to hunt for big cats and described an area in the south where an ample population of leopards and tigers were present. All details from the route to specific dams were described to the two professional poachers and four other members of their community that had been persuaded to join them. The poaching equipment was hidden under the clothing and cloth bundles of women and children and they boarded a train from Delhi in the north down to Karnataka state.

Prayer of the Kalka Mata

The poaching gang made it into the forest and set up 'base camp' in the outskirts of the dam area described by the financier, while the women and children positioned themselves in the streets of the small town begging and selling plastic flowers as a cover for the arrival of this new group.

A few days passed while the group collected provisions and observed the National Park forest guards to determine a suitable time in order to enter the forest. Every detail of the poaching operation was planned, even down to sourcing the khaki shirts of forest guards to avoid detection in the forest.

'You know before we left for the forest on the final day, we even performed a special puja (prayer) of the Kalka Mata, who protects us from the various dangers of the forest. Our people who stay back at the camp continue the daily prayers until we return to ensure that the divine protection remains with us and we're blessed with enough booty,' Dale said with a mouthful of rice.

The illogical nature of this statement, resonated with our team – the poachers pray to the goddess Kalka Mata. Her divine vehicle in the forest is a tiger and this group call on her in order to bless a planned poaching attack on her closest forest ally. He told me how they walked right into the core area of the tiger reserve through the river bed and set up their camp under boulders, approximately 15 kilometres inside the forest.

After three days camping, they selected three spots frequented by tigers – using signs such as pug marks and scratch marks and their honed knowledge to pin-point tiger locales. The plan was to set the traps in all three locations in one day to get three animals in just that much time! This way they could get out of the forest without spending much time after the first kill.

'This is where my role majorly came in. I'm known for skills as a hunter and a skinner, which is why they needed someone like me with them on the trip in the first place. All the traps were set in the three locations, a little distance from each other so that three tigers could be easily trapped. Two of them were placed on paths leading to a small water hole on top of the hill which was the only source of water in the area. The third was placed near the river bed, right next to a tree which bore witness to the assaults of a big tiger,' Singh said as he settled himself more comfortably on the ground.

Detailed planning

There are very few lengths to which poachers won't go to get their kill but the level of detailed planning in this case amazed the investigations team! This was a gang of unassuming men who are illiterate to boot,

World tiger populations

Russia:
420 tigers

China:
30 tigers

Laos, Vietnam
& Cambodia:
30 tigers

Nepal:
120 tigers

India:
1,400 tigers

Malaysia:
500 tigers

Thailand:
200-300 tigers

Indonesia:
400 tigers

Source: Which place will be the first to lose its tigers? WWF 2014

managing to easily travel hundreds of kilometres, into unknown territory, setting up camps inside the forest and almost succeeding in poaching three tigers! They had no guns, just a few necessities.

'Looking at the vast trove of knowledge they have on tracking tigers and leopards,' Jose wondered, 'just how much of a difference these people could make if they ever chose to use it for the right side of the law and conservation?'

Part three

After a few more days and the poachers had re-visited the prepared holes, where fresh pug marks confirmed they had selected the right location. They were ready for the final part of their plan, to set the three traps and catch three animals within just a couple of days so they could quickly leave the area. The traps are placed carefully in the small hole and then camouflaged with dry leaves and grass so it is completely hidden.

A broken twig is placed just inches before the trap. This is because a wild animal will often avoid stepping on a broken twig so they will place their paw just after the twig, exactly where the trap is. They dug holes in the ground to set up the heavy chains which would secure the traps on the ground. The holes measured about two feet deep and each took an hour to dig. While one poacher worked, the other acted as a sentry watching out for the forestry guards, villagers and of course, tigers and elephants.

Fortunately, soon after the traps were laid, an elephant stamped on one of the traps and instead of getting caught, damaged the side lever which secures the jaw when snapped. Despite having spare parts and tools for the repair, the part they had with them did not fit the trap and they were forced to return to their base camp to perform the repair. In the two days that had gone by, they had not caught a single animal. They dismantled the traps and hid them in different locations before going back to their base camp.

Caught by a blanket

This was when they were spotted by the forest staff – who were on high alert. They were detained and questioned, at first using their cover story of impoverishment and travelling to the area to sell plastic flowers for a living. Their personal belongings were examined and at first nothing unusual came out of it, until till part of the jaw trap fell out the blanket! The small piece of iron by itself looked harmless but the range officer recognised it for what it was, and e-mailed the photo to our experts to confirm its use as part of a jaw trap for capturing tigers.

It was now clear to the forest department that they were experienced poachers and that there were traps set in the jungle. After continued questioning, Dale Singh finally relented and admitted to the guards where the traps were hidden. One of the poachers soon corroborated his story and our team were brought in to re-enter the forest and remove the traps.

Dale Singh proceeded to show investigators how the traps had been set giving a live demonstration about how he had camouflaged the deadly trap – when he was done all one could see was a little twig a few inches from the site. Singh told us that the twig was left on purpose and that a tiger or a leopard will inadvertently place their paw on the trap in a bid to avoid stepping on the twig!

The traps are set in the evening and the poachers hide nearby so they can hear when the tiger is trapped. They wait for some time following this so the animal is exhausted and they can approach safely. The animal is then speared through the mouth and left to bleed. This prevents any noise attracting attention and kills the animal faster. It also means the skin has not been damaged in any way, retaining its price. Once the tiger is dead, the skin is removed within half an hour and the body hidden so they can come back later to collect the bones which will boost their profit. The skin is then coated in salt and herbal preparations before being dried.

Dale explained his tactics to avoid capture:

'We only set it up in paths mostly used by the big cats, which are away from the forest staff's patrolling route. There are exclusive tiger paths which are often avoided by other animals and we search for such paths to ensure that we don't catch anything other than a tiger.'

The knowledge displayed by the captured poachers on tracking and identifying recent presence of big cats was astounding to our specialist investigations team and saddening to think this could be a knowledge and skill-set used to conserve rather than poach the tiger.

Skins are transported by the women in the group who hide the skin under their loose clothes as they are unlikely to be searched. They deliberately keep themselves so filthy that no one wants to touch them to avoid frisking during their travels. They almost always travel by train and after arriving at their destination, wait for the middlemen to come and collect the goods, which are taken to the international borders to be sold.

The planning and precautions undertaken by the group are amazing considering the minimum resources available to them. The two men's confessions of targeted tiger poaching corroborated, and over the course of the investigations our undercover team learnt the incredible details of what was uncovered to be a highly planned interstate poaching gang supported by an illegal wildlife criminal network.

For our conservation team their in-depth investigations have gained vital evidence for prosecution and gained greater knowledge of poachers' tactics. The gang of six were eventually convicted as a result of the specialist support of our WTI team. This knowledge is valuable to tiger conservation and criminal investigations work across India and will enable more successful arrests like this one.

⇨ The above information is reprinted with kind permission from Care for the Wild International. Please visit www.careforthewild.com for further information.

© Care for the Wild International 2013

The scale and consequences of the illegal trade in wildlife

The representatives of Governments and Regional Economic Integration Organisations gathered in London on 13 February 2014, recognising the significant scale and detrimental economic, social and environmental consequences of the illegal trade in wildlife.

There is a serious threat to the survival of many species if action is not taken to tackle the illegal wildlife trade. Poaching and trafficking undermines the rule of law and good governance, and encourages corruption. It is an organised and widespread criminal activity, involving transnational networks. The proceeds are in some cases used to support other criminal activities, and have been linked to armed groups engaged in internal and cross-border conflicts. Rangers and others dedicated to protecting wildlife are being killed or injured in significant numbers.

The illegal wildlife trade, and the poaching which feeds it, has in some places reached unprecedented levels. Serious poaching incidents are more frequent, are occurring in areas previously safe from such activity, and are more devastating in scale. Individual poachers or ad hoc gangs are being increasingly replaced by well-resourced and organised groups including transnational criminal networks.

The illegal wildlife trade robs states and communities of their natural capital and cultural heritage, with serious economic and social consequences. It undermines the livelihoods of natural resource dependent communities. It damages the health of the ecosystems they depend on, undermining sustainable economic development. The criminal activity and corruption associated with trafficking restricts the potential for sustainable investment and development which is needed in new economic activities and enterprises.

Decisive and urgent action is now needed to tackle the illegal wildlife trade in endangered fauna and flora. For many species, the illegal trade, and the poaching which fuels it, is an ongoing and growing problem. There has been a particularly dramatic escalation in the rate of poaching of elephants and rhinoceroses in some places in recent years. The severe threat posed to these iconic species is increasingly also a threat to regional security and sustainable development. Action to tackle the illegal trade in elephants and rhinoceroses will strengthen our effectiveness in tackling the illegal trade in other endangered species. Such action will also support the sustainable utilisation of resources.

12–13 February 2014

⇨ The above information is reprinted with kind permission from the Department for Environment, Food & Rural Affairs, Department for International Development, Foreign & Commonwealth Office and Home Office.

Fighting wildlife trafficking online

The Internet is the world's largest marketplace. Un-regulated, anonymous and virtually unlimited in reach, it offers endless opportunities for criminal activities, among them a flourishing illegal trade in protected wildlife. IFAW's investigations of this trade have revealed a shocking array of wildlife and wildlife products for sale online.

Among them:

⇨ Elephant ivory

⇨ Tiger bags, tiger-bone medicine and even a live 'pet' tiger, as well as cheetah coats and leopard skins

⇨ Products made from rhino horns and elephant parts

⇨ Whole shells and jewellery items made from the endangered hawksbill turtle

⇨ An emerging market in endangered birds and their eggs

⇨ Live primates for sale, including one gorilla offered by a seller claiming to be in London, and four baby chimpanzees

⇨ Traditional bear bile medicines 'farmed' in the most cruel ways from the black bear

⇨ Shahtoosh shawls made from the wool of an endangered Tibetan antelope – which the sale or purchase of is illegal

⇨ Live reptiles and their skins, many from endangered or protected species.

IFAW Investigations into online wildlife trade

IFAW's first investigation into Internet trade in 2004 uncovered a thriving trade in ivory in the United Kingdom. A 2007 follow-up report focusing specifically on ivory trade on eBay found 2,275 ivory items for sale on eight national eBay websites in a single week.

IFAW undertook yet another investigation into Internet trade in 2008 into 183 publicly accessible websites in 11 countries, looking at both wildlife product and live animal trade in species on Appendix I of the Convention on International Trade in Endangered Species (CITES) – those most at threat from extinction and that are, or may be affected by trade.

The findings, published in the report *Killing with Keystrokes: An Investigation of the Illegal Wildlife Trade on the World Wide Web (2008)*, recorded a staggering 7,122 online auctions, advertisements and classifieds, with an advertised value of US$3.87 million. The report also identified ivory as a major area for trade, representing more than 73 per cent of the activity monitored.

Shortly after it was revealed in the report that 83 per cent of the ivory items found worldwide in the investigation were for sale on eBay sites, eBay Inc. instituted a global ban on ivory sales on all its websites.

IFAW's ongoing work with other major online marketplaces has resulted in Alibaba (www.taobao.com), the world's largest online business-to-business trading platform for small businesses, and the German sites kleinanzeigen.ebay.de (a subsidiary of eBay), markt.de and hood.de all implementing a ban on all ivory products. Kleinanzeigen.ebay.de also agreed to implement a ban on living specimens listed on CITES Appendix I.

Internet trade in wildlife in Europe

Building upon IFAW's prior research regarding online trade in ivory in Europe, in 2013 INTERPOL released a report regarding an investigation of ivory trade online in nine European countries, called *Project Web*.

During the operation, enforcers reviewed publicly available online advertisements and found hundreds of ivory items conservatively valued at approximately EUR 1,450,000 for sale during a two-week period. As a result of the surveillance, six national and three international investigations were launched in cases where ivory was described as new or where ivory was being traded from abroad.

The *Project Web* report called for new legislation and additional funding to help enforcers crack down on illegal wildlife trade.

Although *Killing with Keystrokes* in 2008 identified the United States as being responsible for more than two-thirds of the online trade in the investigation, three European countries – the UK, France and Germany – when combined, accounted for 15.2 per cent of the total trade in CITES Appendix I species, of which 65 per cent of items were elephant/ivory products.

Killing with Keystrokes, 2.0: IFAW's Investigation into the European Online Ivory Trade revisits three countries noted in our 2008 survey as major contributors to trade online of CITES Appendix 1 species, the UK, France and Germany and two new ones – Portugal and Spain. This report focused on Internet trade in ivory in these countries and the effectiveness of current marketplace restrictions on ivory sales and their enforcement.

Overall, these results show a high volume of trade with hundreds of potentially illegal items offered for sale on websites – predominantly in France, Portugal and Spain – over the survey period.

The total advertised monetary value of all listings was EUR 649,689, although investigators recorded additional advertisements that were lacking any information on prices.

The work goes on

IFAW continues to work with online market providers to raise awareness of the specific problems of online trade in endangered products. This includes encouraging providers to offer more information on their sites to consumers on wildlife and the law, to improve filters and monitoring activities and to institute bans on the sale of wildlife products including ivory. IFAW is also working with some providers who have instituted strict policies to ensure that they have effective and regular enforcement of those policies – a critical factor in preventing unscrupulous buyers from continuing to ply their trade.

Resources

Elephants on the High Street: an investigation into ivory trade in the UK (2004)

Caught in the Web: Wildlife Trade on the Internet (2005)

Bidding for Extinction (2007)

Killing with Keystrokes: An Investigation of the Illegal Wildlife Trade on the World Wide Web (2008)

Killing with Keystrokes, 2.0: IFAW's Investigation into the European Online Ivory Trade (2011)

Project Web: An INTERPOL investigation of ivory trade in nine European countries (2013)

⇨   The above information is reprinted with kind permission from the International Fund for Animal Welfare. Please visit www.ifaw. org for further information.

A speech by The Prince of Wales at the Illegal Wildlife Trade Conference

Secretary of State, Ministers, Your Excellencies, Ladies and Gentlemen, I am enormously grateful to you all I must say for taking the trouble to attend this unbelievably important meeting, as I know that some of you have travelled tremendously long distances and may very well be suffering from some appalling jet lag or other.

I also am hugely grateful to Kate Silverton for giving up her precious time. I know she's taken a huge interest in this particular subject for some time. Having been lucky enough to sit next to her at dinner once or twice I know how much she minds. So it really is very kind of you Kate, today.

I particularly appreciate the fact that Mr Owen Paterson, the Secretary of State for Environment, Food & Rural Affairs has agreed to join me in hosting this meeting, and I also owe a particular debt of gratitude to WWF UK (of which I became President two years ago), as well as to TRAFFIC and the IUCN. Their knowledge and expertise have been invaluable to the members of my ISU (International Sustainability Unit). in putting together this very productive gathering.

Ladies and Gentlemen, the fact that my son is here today, too, in order to support his aging father is hugely appreciated, as I know that his knowledge of, and indeed love for, Africa, its wildlife and its people has not only helped him to understand why this gathering is so important, but has meant that he has already been much involved in the field of conservation with, for instance, the Tusk Trust of which he is patron and indeed other organisations. I'm only sorry of course that my father could not

be here. He of course has been involved for some many years in this whole question of conservation and indeed the relationship between species and their habitats and those communities who depend so much on those habitats and the biodiversity that they provide.

So Ladies and Gentlemen we come together today to find tangible ways to combat the explosion of trafficking in wildlife that has been occurring in recent years. In this room, we have brought together many of the key countries engaged in this battle along with non-governmental and multilateral experts and of course private sector representatives. In convening this particular group, we sought the expertise not only of wildlife conservationists, but also of those with experience in fighting organised crime and promoting national security.

It is particularly important at this crucial time to recognise that illegal trade in wildlife is a serious crime that is not only decimating critically endangered species, but is also a pervasive instrument in destabilising economic and political security. Finding a solution will require people from many different sectors to work together. I would like, if I may, just to take a moment to review what has brought us here. I have already used the words 'combat' and 'battle' and I have barely begun my remarks! I use these words quite intentionally.

We face one of the most serious threats to wildlife ever, and we must treat it as a battle, because it is precisely that. Now many in this room, I know, come from organisations and agencies that are operating in the front line of this battle and I am full of admiration for your heroic efforts in an increasingly dangerous situation. Organised bands of criminals are stealing and slaughtering elephants, rhinoceros and tigers, as well as large numbers of other species, in a way that has never ever been seen before. They are taking these animals, sometimes in unimaginably high numbers, using the weapons of war – assault rifles,

silencers, night vision equipment, and helicopters. And because these criminals must kill the animals to profit from the black market sale of wildlife 'products', they are pushing many species towards extinction at an alarming and unprecedented rate. Experience shows that with the removal of such species it is only a short step, as I'm sure Professor Lee White has explained, to the subsequent removal of their habitat and with it the biodiversity on which we all depend ultimately for our very survival. Organised crime has become heavily involved in the illegal wildlife trade because, quite obviously, there is a lot of money to be made, and the risk of being caught is relatively low.

Skyrocketing demand – primarily, but not exclusively, from Asia – for ivory, rhino horn and tiger parts, as well as other products, is fuelling this astonishing explosion in poaching. The bulk of the intended use is no longer for products that can be classified as traditional medicines. Instead, many more people in the rapidly growing economies are seeking exotic products that reflect their economic prosperity and status.

In this regard, it is clearly vital to tackle the demand for such products amongst consumers by recruiting the help of every form of media to communicate more widely and effectively its disastrous consequences. There are, I see, quite a few representatives of the media here today, so I can only appeal to all your parent companies, networks and agencies to join with us urgently in this battle before it is quite literally too late. Governments, non-governmental organisations and multilateral institutions have been working incredibly hard to fight back. However, despite all of this good work – and despite the conservation efforts of the last several decades – it is clear that new approaches are urgently needed. This situation should be of the deepest concern to all of us and therefore I am immeasurably heartened by your presence here today as it is, at the very least,

encouraging evidence that you recognise the need for urgent action.

And by urgent, I mean urgent! The animals being slaughtered to fuel this entirely unnecessary trade provide many benefits to humans, as well as to those other species that share their habitat. It is surely unthinkable that these creatures, which have roamed the planet for thousands, if not millions, of years, could disappear completely within a decade, or even less. As a father and a soon-to-be grandfather, I find it inconceivable that our children and grandchildren could live in a world bereft of these animals. Humanity is less than humanity without the rest of creation. Their destruction will diminish us all. Perhaps those of us in this room will know how difficult it can be to convince others of the importance of preserving and protecting wildlife and its habitat as part of our heritage and 'natural capital'. How, then, can we encourage more people to share our concern and turn that concern into action?

Well, first of all, perhaps we need to make it clear that the threat to wildlife has also become a threat to the rule of law and to global stability. Wildlife crime alone yields profits of about ten billion US Dollars per year, and often occurs with other crimes, such as corruption, money laundering, passport fraud and murder. The same routes used to smuggle wildlife and wildlife products through countries and across continents are often used to smuggle other contraband, most notably drugs. When the illegal trade in wildlife is coupled with crime involving timber, the illegal trade in flora and fauna is ranked as the fourth biggest transnational crime – with a value of 17 billion US dollars – just behind trafficking in weapons, drugs and people. Increasingly sophisticated, well-financed groups are now doing the poaching, which means it really has become a form of trafficking. In some cases, rebel militias are killing elephants, and when park rangers try to protect the animals from assault, they are often killed too.

Equally disturbing, the profits from wildlife trafficking have in some cases been traced to terrorist groups. So, these are not the local poachers operating alone that countries encountered just a few years ago. Secondly, wildlife trafficking directly threatens economic security. Those who work in tourism – a vitally important industry for many countries – or as park rangers, as well as many other related occupations, depend on healthy populations of wildlife. Their livelihoods are now threatened directly by rampant poaching.

Surely, any one of these arguments should convince more people to enlist in this fight? To borrow a few words from the former Secretary of State, Hillary Clinton – who I know has already done so much to raise the profile of this issue. She said, '…there is something for everyone. If you love animals, if you want a more secure world, if you want our global economy not to be corrupted by this illicit behaviour, there is so much we can do together.'

Ladies and Gentlemen, stamping out the illegal wildlife trade needs to be placed very near the top of the global agenda. And it needs to be addressed by world leaders as

an urgent priority. Indeed, that is the premise of this meeting today, which I am pleased to say, will lead to a meeting of Heads of State this autumn that will be hosted by Her Majesty's Government. Today's meeting is important, therefore, because it will lay the groundwork for the action that world leaders will decide to take in a few months time.

I understand that there have been a number of presentations this morning discussing various solutions to the problem, including the need for stronger law enforcement, campaigns to discourage demand for wildlife and wildlife products, and support for programmes that provide alternatives to poaching. In addition, several speakers mentioned the need for governments to develop an international strategy to combat trafficking and address the issue internally as one of national security. But Ladies and Gentlemen perhaps the most important priority is the reduction of consumer demand in key countries which TRAFFIC and WildAid know only too well since they are working so hard in this crucial field but they clearly need more support from governments and the media.

I know the governments represented here will meet this afternoon to consider these and other ideas. I can only encourage you to be bold and to develop effective, practical solutions for consideration at the Heads of State meeting. Along with so many others who share my concern, I also urge you to act swiftly as we are in a terrible race against time to save species whose loss will be an immeasurable stain on the whole course of human history, as well as an enduring and irreversible tragedy.

Thank you again, Ladies and Gentlemen, for your presence here today and for your commitment to this important issue. I much look forward to hearing the results of your discussions and, after the next meeting, of the commitments made by Heads of State.

21 May 2013

⇨ The above information is reprinted with kind permission from Clarence House. Please visit www.princeofwales.gov.uk for further information.

© Clarence House 2014

Online ivory trade: summary of findings from the IFAW report
Killing with Keystrokes 2.0

	Number websites tracked	Number of ivory ads	% of total ads tracked	Advertised value of all ads (EUR)	Value of final sales recorded (EUR)	% of ads 'Likely Compliant'	% of ads 'Possible Violation'	% of ads 'Likely Violation'
UK	5	61	9%	11,539.80	3,511.40	0	41%	59%
Portugal	13	189	28%	211,666.10	163,815.00	0	82%	18%
Spain	4	118	18%	231,234.00	Not shown	0.90%	30.50%	68.60%
France	14	262	39%	173,374.00	eBay: 30,50	7.25%	5.34%	87.40%
Germany	7	39	6%	21,875.00	N/A	0%	38.50%	61.50%
Totals	**43**	**669**	**100%**	**649,688.90**	**167,356.90**	**N/A**	**N/A**	**N/A**
Percentages						2%	39%	59%

IFAW investigators tracked 669 online auctions and advertisements offering ivory for sale domestically and internationally in the five countries listed above. © IFAW 2011

2013 in review: the year wildlife crime became an international security issue

Jessica Aldred looks back at some of the year's biggest wildlife and natural world stories.

Arguably the biggest story of 2013 was wildlife crime, which escalated from a conservation issue to an international security threat. Driven by rising demand for ivory from east Asia, it has doubled over the past five years into a global trade worth $10 billion, threatening political and economic stability in central Africa.

This month there were warnings that Africa could lose one-fifth of its elephants in the next decade if the continent's poaching crisis is not stopped. By the end of September, a record 704 rhinos had been killed by poachers in South Africa and 47 in Kenya this year. Figures showed two-thirds of forest elephants had been killed by ivory poachers in the past decade.

Some high-profile massacres hit the headlines, with 86 elephants – including 33 pregnant females – killed in less than a week in Chad, 26 elephants slaughtered at a wildlife-viewing site in the Central African Republic and 80 poisoned at a water hole in Zimbabwe.

While conservation groups looked to technology such as surveillance drones and GPS trackers to aid their efforts, park rangers lost lives and faced corruption fighting a one-sided war against increasingly militarised and organised gangs of poachers sometimes linked to terrorist groups like Al-Shabaab.

With Prince Charles and his son the Duke of Cambridge calling for a 'war on poachers', UK Prime Minister David Cameron announced he would host the highest level global summit to date on combating the illegal wildlife trade. In the US, the Obama administration said it would destroy all six million tonnes of its ivory stocks and the Philippines crushed five million tonnes of seized ivory beneath industrial rollers.

In 2013 the weather played a big part for British wildlife, with a wet winter, a 'delayed spring' and hot summer affecting both flora and fauna. As the cold spell continued into April, conservationists warned hedgehogs, birds, insects, reptiles and frogs were all struggling.

In May, the National Trust embarked on a census to discover whether puffin numbers had plummeted after a year of extreme weather, and the UK barn owl population was reported to have suffered its worst breeding season for more than 30 years after a run of extreme weather events. The erratic weather had a knock-on effect later in the year with species like wasps and butterflies being seen a month later than usual.

Decline was a word used frequently throughout 2013 when it came to talking about wildlife in the UK and around the world. The significant *State of Nature* report, published in May, found that more than half of UK wildlife species are in decline. In October an audit of more than 200 native UK species – including birds, bats, moths, butterflies, hares and dormice – showed that priority species have declined on average by 58% since 1970.

Europe's grassland butterfly population has plummeted in the past two decades, new research published in 2013 showed, with a near halving in the numbers of key species since 1990. And after the miserable summer of 2012, there were fewer butterflies in British skies in 2013 than for thousands of years, leaving several species in danger of extinction from parts of the country. British moths are also in calamitous decline, a major report showed in February, declining in southern Britain by 40% over 40 years.

In British waterways, a new five-year survey found that the water vole – the creature immortalised as Ratty in *The Wind in the Willows* – is vanishing from the British countryside, with the population slumping by more than one-fifth.

More than 4,000 birds of at least 18 species washed up dead or were affected by a sticky substance covering beaches from Cornwall to Dorset in two separate incidents in January and April this year.

There were mixed fortunes for bird populations in 2013. In December, the authoritative *State of the UK's Birds* report concluded that some of Britain's most familiar countryside birds have plummeted in numbers since the 1990s, with some species disappearing altogether from parts of the UK. The report drew heavily on the British Trust for Ornithology's mammoth volunteer-led project the *Bird Atlas 2007-11*, published a month earlier. The new atlas of 1,300 maps shows the patterns of distribution, abundance and change among 296 bird species in Britain and Ireland.

In October, statistics showed the number of wild birds in the UK was still falling, and among garden birds, starlings, house sparrows and other threatened species suffered further declines.

The decline in birds of prey continued, with the hen harrier failing to breed in England this summer for the first time since the 1960s. The species now stands on the brink of extinction, with rogue grouse moor gamekeepers blamed for their decline.

Cases of the illegal persecution of British birds is continuing to rise, a December report from the RSPB showed, with 208 reports of the shooting and destruction of birds of prey in 2012. It is hoped legal changes that will be debated in Parliament next year will introduce stricter penalties for wildlife crimes.

The fortunes of the house sparrow seemed to be changing in 2012, however, with figures in September showing that the decline in their numbers appears to have levelled off.

In April, the European Union suspended the use of three neonicotinoid pesticides linked to serious harm in bees, despite the opposition of the UK ministers. In June the UK Government launched an 'urgent' review of the crisis facing bees and other pollinators in the UK and pledged to introduce a national pollinator strategy.

In August, the controversial badger cull went ahead – amid protests – in Gloucestershire and west Somerset, in two pilot schemes attempting to stop the spread of bovine tuberculosis in cattle. Despite the cull being extended, it failed to reach its target, meaning it was 'very likely' that the risk of tuberculosis in cattle had gone up, not down, according to an expert.

British trees were under attack in 2013 from a variety of threats including sweet chestnut blight, the oak processionary moth caterpillar, and one year after it broke out in the UK, ash dieback disease. Britain's 80 million ash trees remain at deadly risk from ash dieback caused by *Chalara fraxinea*, a virulent fungal disease that has swept across Europe. Latest figures from the Forestry Commission reported a total of 613 sightings in nurseries, plantations and established woodland around the UK.

In October the St Jude storm that swept across England was estimated to have killed around ten million trees.

Internationally, destruction of the Amazon rainforest increased by almost one-third in the past year, reversing a decade-long trend of better protection for the world's greatest rainforest.

But almost 200,000 hectares of Tasmania's old growth forest were world heritage-listed in 2013, bringing hope that a three-decade fight between environmentalists, politicians and loggers is over.

Internationally, the CITES international wildlife summit in Bangkok awarded protection against the finning trade to five shark species, but failed to halt the polar bear trade. Iceland resumed its commercial hunting of fin whales after a two-year suspension.

In November, the IUCN published its annual 'red list'. The latest update of endangered species showed worrying declines for the okapi, the white-winged flufftail, the red belly toad, Caribbean skinks and the martial eagle. Another study published by the IUCN this year showed that nearly one in five of the world's estimated 10,000 species of lizards, snakes, turtles, crocodiles and other reptiles are threatened with extinction.

Talks to create the world's two largest marine reserves in the Antarctic broke down in November for the third time in a year, with conservationists branding Russia a 'repeat offender' for blocking an international agreement. In the UK, ministers named 27 new marine conservation zones in November to protect seahorses, coral reefs, oyster beds and other marine life – four less than ministers proposed and far short of the 127 zones recommended by the Government's own consultation.

A hard-fought battle over European Union fisheries policy saw the ending of the wasteful practice of fish discards, with an agreement signed to gradually phase out the practice – where unwanted fish are thrown back into the sea – from 2015 to 2019. The Fish Fight campaign by Hugh Fearnley-Whittingstall, the chef and *Guardian* food writer, was cited by the European commission as a key factor in winning the battle.

The discovery of new species made for some welcome respite from the bad news. In October, a leaf-tail gecko, a golden-coloured skink and a boulder-dwelling frog were three new species discovered in a 'lost world' in northern Queensland, Australia. In Suriname, scientists discovered 60 species new to science, including a chocolate-coloured frog and a tiny dung beetle

less than 3 mm long. A purring monkey, a vegetarian piranha and a flame-patterned lizard were among more than 400 new species of animals and plants that have been discovered in the past four years in the Amazon rainforest, conservationists say.

And there were other good news stories. Sightings of the variable harlequin toad (*Atelopus varius*) – thought to be extinct in Costa Rica – led researchers to believe other isolated fragments of Central America's disappearing amphibians may survive in regions scourged by the deadly chytrid fungus disease.

One of the world's most elusive wild cats, the Bornean bay cat (*Pardofelis badia*) was captured on camera in a heavily logged area of Borneo rainforest together with four other endangered species, suggesting that some wildlife can survive in highly disturbed forests.

In September, a landmark project to reintroduce the extinct short-haired bumblebee (*Bombus subterraneus*) to the UK celebrated its first milestone after experts confirmed that queens had nested and produced young.

Spain's endangered Iberian lynx was brought back from the brink of extinction thanks to an imaginative conservation programme that has brought hunters, farmers and the tourist industry under its wing.

And beaver, bison and eagles were named among the species that have made a successful comeback in Europe in the past 50 years, according to a major survey published in September.

16 December 2013

Ten things you need to know about elephant poaching

It is a familiar cause, but it has never been more urgent. Last year, tens of thousands of Africa's elephants were killed to supply illegal ivory to markets throughout the world. Increasingly, revenue generated from this blood ivory is being used to fuel war and terrorism in Africa.

This year, our Christmas campaign aims to help put a stop to illegal elephant poaching. To find out what all the fuss is about, read our list of the ten things you need to know about the elephant poaching crisis.

1. Big business

Wildlife hunting is big business – a recent 2013 estimate valued the illegal poaching trade in Africa as being worth $17 billion a year and growing.

2. Big weapons

The most common poaching gun in east Africa is the AK47. Increasingly, poachers spot elephant herds from helicopter and target their prey from above. On-the-ground poachers have been known to use machetes, spears and watermelons spiked with cyanide.

3. Big profits

According to gun policy officials the going rate for a rifle in Kenya is around $100–120 – a fortune by local economic standards but a mere fraction of the money that can be made from just one elephant (a single tusk can be worth up to $240).

4. Chinese prices

In China such a tusk would sell for more than $2,000 – its value therefore increasing tenfold by the time it is shipped out of Africa and arrives in Asia.

5. Local misunderstanding

A recent study cited by *The Times* found that less than a third of Chinese people surveyed knew that elephants are killed for their tusks.

6. Common mythology

A separate study showed 70 per cent think they grow back like fingernails. Another myth propagated is that elephants' tusks fall out naturally.

7. 104 deaths a day

Animal rights groups estimate that poachers in Africa kill between 25,000 and 35,000 elephants annually – meaning about 104 die a day.

8. An offence without prosecution

Of the 157 poaching-related cases detected in Kenya in the past three years, less than five per cent have been prosecuted and only three of those convicted were sentenced to jail.

9. Pulverising the trade

The Obama administration destroyed the US reserve of elephant tusks on 5 November 2013 – announcing that the pulverising of 6 tons (5.4 tonnes) of 'blood ivory' would send out the right message to the world.

10. Not far from human

Elephants are more like us than you may know. They can be gay, left-handed, have the ability to grieve and – true to reputation – have amazing memories.

4 December 2013

⇨ The above information is reprinted with kind permission from *The Independent*. Please visit www.independent.co.uk for further information.

© independent.co.uk

One way to fight terrorism?
End the ivory trade

By Peter Seligmann

Recently, I had the honour of taking part in an extraordinary event at the annual meeting of the Clinton Global Initiative (CGI) where nations and NGOs made a historic commitment to end elephant poaching by stopping the killing, stopping the trafficking and stopping the demand for ivory.

Wildlife trafficking is currently the fifth most profitable illegal trade (after drugs, human trafficking, oil theft and counterfeiting). Ivory is one of the most valuable wildlife products on the black market; it's currently valued at more than US$1,000 a pound. In addition, it is virtually untraceable – as the domestic trade of ivory is still legal in some countries, it's nearly impossible to tell its source or legality.

The illegal wildlife trade is a stark example of the direct connection between natural resources and both US and global security. Wildlife trafficking, a $7–10 billion enterprise, funds terrorist groups like the Lord's Resistance Army in Uganda, Darfur's Janjaweed militia and Al-Shabab, the Somalian terrorist group responsible for last month's horrific murders at a Nairobi shopping mall.

Former Secretary of State Hillary Rodham Clinton has been instrumental in bringing this issue to the world stage and highlighting the devastating impact poaching and wildlife trafficking have on African nations, as well as on world security. Her passion and dedication to stopping trafficking was evident earlier this year when she engaged in a discussion at our New York dinner with Conservation International (CI) Vice Chair Harrison Ford, and spoke so eloquently about the devastation caused by traffickers who now arrive equipped with automatic rifles and other advanced technology.

Secretary Clinton and Clinton Foundation Vice-Chair Chelsea Clinton were responsible for bringing us together to commit to stopping wildlife trafficking. They deserve our thanks and gratitude for putting this issue on the CGI agenda.

The current status of global elephant populations is unquestionably bleak. Last year alone, 35,000 elephants were brutally slaughtered for the ivory trade. If poaching continues at its current rate, the forest elephants of the Congo Basin are predicted to become extinct within a decade.

The frightening escalation of elephant poaching in recent years is largely due to increasingly sophisticated technology. These days, poachers associated with criminal groups use helicopters, AK-47s, night vision goggles and other tools to find and kill elephants more quickly and to avoid detection. Facing such high-tech forces, park rangers and guards (who are often unarmed) don't stand a chance. About 1,000 park guards have been killed over the last ten years.

What we're seeing here is the perfect storm of extinction, poverty and radicalism. We're seeing the deterioration of societies and a massive threat to the stability of not only African nations but the entire world. A crucial step in changing this equation is to ensure that the ivory trade comes to an end.

At the CGI meeting, CI and four other organisations – the Wildlife Conservation Society, the African Wildlife Foundation, the International Fund for Animal Welfare and WWF – made a joint commitment of $80 million over three years to fight elephant poaching in three ways: stop the killing, stop the trafficking and stop the demand.

We have defined some really clear benchmarks, ranging from hiring 3,100 new park guards to deploying sniffer dogs at ten key transit points to launching communications campaigns in the countries with the largest markets for ivory. (You may be surprised to learn that the United States is the second-largest market for ivory, after China.)

I believe that the area where CI can make a particularly important contribution is in fighting ivory trafficking. We need to work closely with our friends in African nations to assist them in developing strategies for enforcement for tracking illegal ivory and blocking its sale.

While I look forward to CI's engagement in this critical initiative, I am glad to see African nations taking ownership of this problem. Many of these nations have recognised and are concerned about the future of their elephants, which are valued economic assets.

Wildlife tourism is estimated to make up 20–40% of all international tourism; in Africa in particular, it provides a promising economic opportunity for impoverished communities. And when you lose your elephants to poachers, the vast majority of the people – as well as the nation as a whole – don't benefit.

President Ian Khama of Botswana, whom CI is privileged to have on our board of directors, has seen that depending upon wildlife guards to be effective responders to sophisticated international criminal networks is not effective. That's why his government has set up a national security force that engages the country's entire military in fighting poaching. This initiative has been relatively effective to date, but President Khama worries that Botswana's comparatively large elephant population will become more of a target.

This week in Botswana, CI, the United Nations Development Programme and the World Bank convened government ministers from several African countries to advance the Gaborone Declaration – a set of principles and goals aiming to better acknowledge the value and contribution that nature makes to the health of African states. Part of the conversation was about setting up a shared training programme about how to engage national security forces to fight poaching.

At the CGI event, a number of African nations called for moratoria on the sale of ivory until the African elephant population has sufficiently recovered. In doing so, they are essentially saying, 'We want to solve this problem; it is essential to the future of our people.'

These countries are the backbone of this movement, but they need help from the rest of us – partner governments, NGOs, businesses and individuals – to help them get there.

8 October 2013

⇨ The above information is reprinted with kind permission from Conservation International. Please visit www.conservation.org for further information.

- **In 2012, approximately 34,000 kg of ivory was seized worldwide.**

- **Between October 2012 and January 2013, 12 tonnes of ivory were seized in just four incidents.**

- **In January 2014, a Chinese ivory smuggler was fined £138,000 and will serve a seven-year prison sentence if he is unable to pay the fine.**

Source: ITV News, 10 Jan 2013. Information taken from the Kenya Wildlife Service, National Geographic, International Fund for Animal Welfare and the campaign group Blood Ivory.

Breakthrough as plantation workers jailed for killing orangutan

Conservationists in Sabah in Malaysia are celebrating a breakthrough sentence which has seen two palm oil plantation workers jailed for two years for killing an orangutan. The Sabah Wildlife Department have also described the sentence as a 'landmark decision'.

The two workers pleaded guilty to killing the great ape with a parang – or machete type knife – at Felda Sahabat on 29 January 2014. They claimed they killed the orangutan because it had damaged palm oil plants.

The Sabah Wildlife Department disputed this and said the workers were poaching the animal for the bush meat trade.

Assistant director Dr Sen Nathan from the department said that there was a local demand for bush meat of all types.

The Borneo orangutan (*Pongo pygmaeus*) is classified as endangered and numbers are thought to have fallen on the island by about 50% in the last 60 years.

The Bornean orangutan is endemic to the island of Borneo where it is present in the two Malaysian states of Sabah and Sarawak, as well as in three of the four Indonesian Provinces of Kalimantan.

The last academic survey of Borneo orangutans took place over ten years ago between 2000 and 2003 and numbers were estimated to be between 45,000 and 65,000. Conservationists believe that current numbers or substantially below these estimates due to large-scale habitat loss over the last ten years and increasing threats from poaching and the pet trade.

15 February 2014

⇨ The above information is reprinted with kind permission from *Wildlife News*. Please visit www. wildlife.co.uk for further information.

Chapter 3

Wildlife conservation

International protection of nature and wildlife

Not all threats to wildlife and nature can be tackled at the national level and international cooperation is required to combat these threats and provide greater protection for wildlife and their habitats. Examples where international cooperation offer the best form of protection include combating illegal international trade in endangered species, protection of migratory species and their habitats and tackling climate change and its negative impact on nature and wildlife.

A number of multilateral conventions (international agreements made between several countries) have been developed to protect habitats and wildlife.

Ramsar Convention on Wetlands of international importance especially as Waterfowl Habitat 1971

The purpose of the Convention is to stem the progressive encroachment on and loss of wetlands now and in the future. It seeks to promote the wise use of wetlands, encourage research and promote training in research and the management of wetlands. It also requires contracting parties to designate suitable wetlands to be included in the list of wetlands of international importance. Designated sites in the UK include Morecambe Bay, Avon Valley, Dorset Heathlands and the Severn Estuary. All designated Ramsar sites are also SSSIs. Most of them overlap with Natura 2000 sites. The Convention's obligations are met primarily by means of the Wildlife and Countryside Act 1981 as amended and the equivalent

devolved legislation, and the associated government policies. As a matter of policy Ramsar sites are given the same protection as Natura 2000 sites.

The Convention for the Protection of the World Cultural and Natural Heritage 1972

The World Heritage Convention seeks the identification, protection and conservation of cultural and natural heritage of global importance. Each State party to the Convention may nominate a possible site together with the appropriate management plan, for consideration by the Convention secretariat. The UK has a handful of natural sites namely St Kilda (also of cultural importance); Giants Causeway; Dorset and East Devon coast; Henderson Island (a part of the Pitcairn group of islands) and Gough Island (a part of the Tristan da Cunha group of islands).

Convention on International Trade in Endangered Species of Wild Fauna and Flora (CITES) 1973

The Convention seeks to regulate the international trade in endangered animals and plants and in products derived from them. CITES protected species include whales, dolphins and porpoises, sea turtles, parrots, corals, cacti, aloes, corrals, and orchids. The UK meets its obligations under the Convention by means of the Endangered Species (import and Export) Act 1976. At a European level the provisions of the Convention are met by means of the Control of Trade in Endangered Species Regulation (EEC 338/97). You can find more information on how CITES is enforced in the UK in the Defra website.

Convention on the Conservation of Migratory Species of Wild Animals (CMS or Bonn Convention) 1979

The aim of the Bonn Convention is to conserve migratory species by ensuring that Contracting Parties take the necessary action, individually and collectively, to avoid species becoming endangered. The UK meets its obligations under the Convention by means of Part I of the Wildlife and Countryside Act 1981 as amended and the equivalent devolved legislation.

Convention on the Conservation of European Wildlife and Natural Habitats (Bern Convention) 1979

The Bern Convention seeks to conserve wild flora and fauna and their natural habitats and to promote European cooperation in this area. It gives special attention to endangered and vulnerable species, including endangered and vulnerable migratory species. Although it primarily operates at the European regional level, it extends to some parts of Africa, including Burkina Faso, Tunisia, Morocco and Senegal which are state parties to the Convention. The Bern Convention is enforced in the UK through the Wildlife and Countryside Act 1981.

UN Convention on the Law of the Sea (UNCLOS) 1982

UNCLOS provides the legal framework for international governance of seas and oceans. Although not primarily concerned with the protection of wildlife and nature, it does require states to promote peaceful use of the seas and oceans and equitable and efficient utilisation of their resources. Some of the provisions of UNCLOS that affect nature and wildlife, include the duty to prevent, reduce and control marine pollution and coastal states' responsibilities to conserve and manage resources in their respective exclusive economic zones (EEZ). UNCLOS also allows for the protection of cetaceans and other marine mammals in the high seas.

Convention on Biological Diversity (CBD)1992

The objectives of the Convention are the conservation of biological diversity; the sustainable use of

its components; and the fair and equitable sharing of the benefits of utilising the genetic resource. Amongst other things, the Convention requires parties to draw up plans for conservation and sustainable use of biological diversity. The UK meets this obligation by means of Biodiversity Action Plans. This is a policy driven initiative. Public bodies have a general duty with regard to biodiversity as set out in the Natural Environment and Rural Communities Act 2006 (England and Wales), the Nature Conservation

(Scotland) Act 2004 and the Wildlife and Natural Environment (Northern Ireland) Act 2011.

⇨ The above information is reprinted with kind permission from UK Environmental Law Association. Please visit www.environmentlaw. org.uk for further information.

£1.3 million Government pledge to protect our most endangered species

This new fund cements the UK's commitment to leading the way in international conservation.

£1.3 million is being invested in a range of projects dedicated to protecting some of the world's most endangered and best-loved species, Environment Minister Richard Benyon announced today.

From supporting efforts to stamp out the barbaric trade in rhino horn to preserving habitats for fast-disappearing wild tigers, this new fund cements the UK's commitment to leading the way in international conservation.

Environment Minister Richard Benyon said:

'Global action must be taken before these species are wiped out for good. Tigers, rhinos, elephants and apes are much loved animals that some of us take for granted. Yet many are suffering horrific deaths at the hands of poachers and traffickers or because their habitats are being destroyed.

'It would be a travesty if these animals were allowed to disappear forever, which is why the UK Government is committed to leading the way in supporting such vital international conservation.

'We need to stop these animals disappearing forever and the projects receiving funding today are working to do just that, which is why I am so pleased to be able to support them.'

Defra has consistently supported efforts to protect tigers and rhinos in the wild, earlier this year pledging over a quarter of a million pounds to a range of conservation projects. This latest funding will go towards efforts to clamp down on the international trade in endangered species and to the Global Tiger Recovery Plan, which is working to double the number of the animals in the wild by 2022.

The £1.3 million fund will contribute to vital projects across the world to help animals that are on the brink of extinction have a chance of survival.

A breakdown of the projects receiving funding are:

⇨ £312k – Global Tiger Recovery Programme – a global programme, running until 2022, being coordinated by the World Bank;

⇨ £312k – Contribution to the Nagoya Protocol Implementation;

⇨ £200k – UK – Brazil workshop to develop biodiversity actions plans for countries across the world;

- £120k – Zoological Society of London – Progressing REDD+ as a sustainable funding mechanism for tiger conservation in the Berbak National Park;

- £100k – ABS Collaborative initiative with Colombia – to pursue an initiative on biodiversity with the Colombians;

- £100k – The Great Apes Survival Project – shaping a new strategy for protecting this vulnerable species;

- £50k – IUCN African elephant (AfESG) specialist group – AfESG work with African states on elephant conservation including the fight against poaching and illegal trade;

- £50k – IUCN African rhino (AfRSG) specialist group. AfRSG work with African states on rhino conservation;

- £40K – To strengthen Convention on International Trade in Endangered Species (CITES) implementation via the International Consortium for Combating Wildlife Crime;

- £25k – Flagship Species Fund an additional contribution to the £100k already given to Fauna and Flora International to support small-scale biodiversity projects around the world;

- £14k – Rhino conservation to a number of vital rhino conservation missions;

- £14k – Ivory action plan verification missions to combat the illegal trade in ivory; and

- £10k – Zoological Society of London – fire fighting in Berbak National Park, to help safeguard a key tiger habitat.

30 December 2011

- The above information is reprinted with kind permission from the Department for Environment, Food & Rural Affairs. Please visit www.gov.uk for further information.

Hunter Melissa Bachman sparks fury after posing with dead lion

By Sara C Nelson

Animal lovers are up in arms after a woman describing herself as a 'hardcore huntress' posted images of herself holding a rifle and beaming as she posed with the body of a lion she had apparently just killed.

Melissa Bachman – whose open Facebook page also boasts images of her with numerous other dead trophies – wrote of the image: 'An incredible day hunting in South Africa!! Stalked inside 60-yards on this beautiful male lion...what a hunt!'

The post adds the picture was taken at South Africa's Maroi Conservancy.

Bachman's official website tells of a childhood of hunting and an early career in TV broadcasting and producing.

After travelling the world 'filming a variety of incredible hunters', it adds Bachman 'still longed for the day she could be the one squeezing the trigger'.

Bachman's dreams came true and she now produces, writes and hunts on camera for her show *Winchester Deadly Passion*.

The images of Bachman posing with the lion were posted on 1 November but have gone viral in recent days, culminating in an online petition calling on the government of South Africa to deny her future entry to the country.

Close to 90,000 people have signed the Change.org document, which describes Bachman as 'an absolute contradiction to the culture of conservation'.

The letter, addressed to Mkuseli Apleni, director general of South Africa's Department of Home Affairs, Bomo Edna Molewa at the Ministry of Water and Environmental Affairs, and Lakela Kaunda from the private office of the president, adds: 'Her latest Facebook post features her with a lion which she has just executed and murdered in our country.

'As tax payers we demand she no longer be granted access to this country and its natural resources.'

Bachman is no stranger to controversy – last year she was dropped from the National Geographic series *Ultimate Survival Alaska* – after a petition blasted her for being a 'contracted trophy killer'.

The petition received more than 13,000 signatures in less than 24 hours.

There has been no response from Bachman on this latest petition as yet and the facility to contact her through her website was also disabled at time of press. *HuffPost UK* has contacted her via other means and we await her response.

18 November 2013

- The above information is reprinted with kind permission from *Huffington Post UK*. Please visit www.huffingtonpost.co.uk for further information.

Hunting lions: unpalatable but necessary for conservation?

Text © Luke Hunter, President of Panthera

The mere concept of shooting a big cat in the name of 'sport' nauseates me. I have spent my career working to conserve the world's great cats, and have logged thousands of hours in their magnificent presence. When I watch a male lion grooming his cubs or see a female leopard haul a carcass her own weight up a thorn tree, I am bewildered that some people take pleasure in killing their kind with a high-powered rifle. I'm not especially averse to culling – like all wildlife biologists, my work occasionally necessitates killing animals, such as euthanizing injured wildlife- but it certainly isn't fun. I simply do not understand what drives a hunter to shoot a creature as magnificent as a lion for a trophy and bragging rights.

©Luke Hunter/Panthera

Consequently, I should be delighted at the recent petition to list the African lion as Endangered under the Endangered Species Act. Submitted by a consortium of Washington-based wildlife and animal welfare organisations, the petition argues that legal trophy hunting of lions – mainly by American hunters – is now a leading threat to the species in Africa. If successful, adding the lion to the ESA would most likely prohibit Americans bringing their skins and skulls back to the US. It would not prevent hunters going on safari to kill a lion but very few will bother if they cannot bring home some reminder to hang on the wall.

There is absolutely no doubt that far too many lions are being shot for sport. The process of approving the numbers for hunting (technically, the legal quota that can be exported by hunters) has long been flawed by shoddy science, population estimates which are little better than guesswork, and relentless lobbying by the hunting industry which is powerful, rich and persuasive. Hunting not only risks killing too many lions but it also disrupts the species' complicated social structure. Prime male lions – the most sought after trophies – guard their females from pride take-overs by strange males. Take-overs are catastrophic to lionesses because victorious, incoming males kill any cubs belonging to the previous pride males; infanticide hastens the females' return to estrus, giving the new males their own opportunity to sire cubs. It is a natural part of lion society but excessive hunting removes too many males, too quickly, and the essential protection that males provide which allows females to raise a generation of cubs. Between shooting adults and the related loss of cubs, poorly regulated hunting drives lion declines; it is unequivocal.

But, as counter-intuitive as it first seems, that does not mean that all hunting is necessarily bad for lions. In principle, hunting can be sustainable. That's a relatively straightforward, scientific question, just as it is for any 'harvest', whether for pine trees, sardines or lions. Provided that hunting removes essentially the same

©Luke Hunter/Panthera

proportion and segment of the population that would die naturally, its effect can be neutral. We know that the worst effects of lion hunting can be mitigated by setting very low quotas and also raising age limits to ensure that only older male lions are targeted. And, critically, for us to even consider whether a lion population could be hunted, it must be vigorously insulated from other human threats such as poaching with wire snares and poisoning by local herders. It is an absurd argument mounted by hunters that they should be allowed to shoot a few lions when more are being killed by local people. Predictably, there is little evidence of the hunting industry either providing adequate protection of lion populations, or of embracing more conservative quotas of lions they are permitted to hunt. But there are a handful of exceptions who have done so, showing that hunting does not inevitably come with costs to lion numbers.

More surprisingly, it has the potential to actually conserve lion populations. In Africa, sport hunting is the main revenue earner for large tracts of wilderness outside national parks and reserves. Many such areas are too remote, undeveloped or disease-ridden for the average tourist, precluding their use for photographic safaris. Hunting survives because hunters are usually more tolerant of hardship, and they pay extraordinary sums – up to US$125,000 – to shoot a male lion. The business requires only a handful of rifle-toting visitors to prosper which, in principle, helps protect those areas. The presence of hunting provides African governments with the economic argument to leave safari blocks as wilderness. Without it, cattle and crops – and the almost complete loss of wildlife they

bring – start looking pretty attractive.

Which is why I'm concerned about the ESA petition. If American hunters, by far the largest market for big game safaris in Africa, can no longer hunt, lions and other wildlife will probably lose out, at least in some areas. As unpalatable as it may be, until we find alternative mechanisms to generate the hard cash required to protect wilderness in Africa, hunting is still an alternative we need to consider.

Let me state it again; I think sport-hunting big cats is repellent and I would welcome its demise. The thought of it literally makes me sick to the stomach. But my personal revulsion for hunting won't help lions if shutting it down actually removes protection from African wilderness. Whatever one's personal feeling, hunting should be regarded as yet another tool in the arsenal of options we have to consider if we are to conserve the lion. Without doubt, the entire process that allows hunting big cats in Africa needs a complete overhaul to purge its widespread excesses and enforce far stricter limits on which lions can be hunted and how many. That would force hunters to produce the conservation benefits of which they constantly boast but only rarely produce.

⇨ The above information is reprinted with kind permission from Panthera. Please visit www. panthera.org for further information.

© Panthera 2014

'We need to abolish all zoos,' says Britain's most famous zoo owner Damian Aspinall

One of Britain's most famous wildlife park owners has called on the Government to help him realise his long-term dream – to abolish all zoos.

By Ted Jeory

Damian Aspinall wants his own industry phased out over the next 20–30 years, saying it was wrong to keep sentient creatures as lifelong 'prisoners without parole'.

He said: 'We've played God once when we took animals out of the forest for zoos, so surely we can play God again and try to get some of these animals home.'

Some 80 per cent of zoo animals are not in any sense endangered, he argued, adding they were either hybrid creatures with no conservation value, or on the contraceptive pill to stop them breeding and thereby pushing up costs.

Mr Aspinall, 53, said the millions of pounds spent on new enclosures could be better used breeding endangered species for a return to the wild.

It is a policy he has successfully followed at his Port Lympne and Howletts wild animal parks in Kent where he says 'animals come first'.

A decision to rent out nearby land to two music festivals at Port Lympne, as reported in the *Sunday Express* last year, was a 'mistake', he added.

The Aspinall Foundation, founded by his late father John, the famous casino tycoon and close friend of Lord Lucan, has just returned nine gorillas to the jungle in The Gabon, a moment he described as 'beautiful'.

'They just walked into the forest and started exploring,' he said.

'If you're a true conservationist and you truly believe in nature, the ultimate goal is you don't need zoos.

'They always throw education back at you though, but that's total and utter nonsense.

'In the next 20–30 years, it would be a lovely goal to see zoos phased out or if they're not, to see them truly doing what I believe is true conservation work.

'What I mean by that is that they only keep truly endangered animals.

'Zoos are stuck in a trap because they need to get the public in because otherwise they will go bust.

'And the only way they can get the public in is because the public is simply addicted to animal shows: they demand to see animals on display.

'But truthfully, if zoos did what was best for the animals, not what's best for the public, they would be very different places.

'I absolutely feel sick in my stomach that zoos do animal shows.

'I come from a point of view where no animal should be here to entertain us.

'We're supposed to be the intelligent species: surely we're above having animals entertain our children.

'What we're doing is culturalising our children to say it's OK that man is the dominant species.

'It's just wrong. We need to de-culturalise the public and phase zoos out.

'There's a role for the Government in this.'

However, the British and Irish Association of Zoos and Aquariums said its members already carry out 'significant' conservation work in the wild.

'Captive populations can be used as advocates for conservation and environmental issues by raising awareness, and could one day be returned to their natural habitat, should this be appropriate,' its website adds.

21 July 2013

⇨ The above information is reprinted with kind permission from the *Sunday Express*. Please visit www.express.co.uk for further information.

Do elephants deserve foreign aid?

By Philip Mansbridge, CEO of Care for the Wild International

Zac Goldsmith MP is calling on the UK government to release some of its billions of 'Foreign Aid' money to help stop the decimation of wildlife in developing nations.

We at Care for the Wild helped to draft the wording of Zac's Early Day Motion (EDM) and fully support it, but why?

Surely Foreign Aid is meant to save humans, not animals? So the question is – how can saving an elephant help a human?

Basically, wildlife and humans need each other – they always have and they always will, but not always for the right reasons. Right now in Africa, an elephant is killed for its tusks every 15 minutes – around 40,000 each year – for a lovely trinket to adorn someone's mantel piece, or to be used as chopsticks, jewellery or a business gift to prove stature.

It's not just elephants. This year in South Africa alone, some 900 rhinos have been killed for their horn – this compares with 668 last year (and by way of comparison of just how severe the issue has got over recent years, this is an increase of over 6,000% since 2005). All these precious rhinos dead, just to show wealth in Vietnam, or simply just to look cool curing a hangover.

And it's not just the "flagship" species – you name it, someone (in fairness, mostly someone in China) – consumes it – tiger bones, lion bones, bear bile, reptiles, pangolins, the list goes on.

But to go back to the original question, why does this matter for humans, many of whom are in desperate need of health provisions, education, water and more?

Quite simply because, as the figures so clearly reflect, poaching has moved on.

We're not talking about the select band of rich Westerners, predominantly from the States, who pay large sums of money to kill beautiful endangered animals. (Note: paying $150,000 to shoot a defenceless animal does NOT make you a man, it doesn't make you brave and it doesn't prove your hunting prowess – it just makes you look simple, arrogant, and in need of a serious self-esteem boost.)

We're talking about the poachers who are now being funded and supported by large organised gangs. This criminality is seeping into communities, it is destroying tourism income for local people, it's helping corruption at high levels and it's stopping nations across Africa from moving forward.

Plus, it's killing people – in large numbers. Reported ranger killings over the last ten years have reached over 1,000, plus thousands more are estimated to have been killed locally. Terrorism is also linked – there is strong evidence suggesting that Al Shabaab, the group behind the Nairobi attacks – get funding from poaching.

What's also significant is that wildlife charities like ours are increasingly going beyond wildlife protection to achieve their aims as we recognise that engagement and buy in from the communities is the only way to achieve long-term complex objectives.

As an example, we just purchased text books and stationery for two schools in Kenya as part of our Youth Wildlife Ambassadors programme – to enhance their opportunities in the future and keep them away from the temptation to poach, which is often driven by the lack of education and opportunities. We also support a variety of projects that directly help communities – offering alternative income streams, education, healthcare and more.

With it now formally recognised by the UN that illegal wildlife crime is the fourth biggest illegal global trade by value in the world (at around $20 billion per annum), it's hats off to Zac, as what he has done in submitting this EDM is to call time on the attitude that wildlife crime only affects animals. It doesn't – it's destroying people too.

And we're not talking ridiculous numbers: just a fraction of the UK's international aid budget could make significant dents in wildlife crime. So whether you care about wildlife, or people, or both, I hope you realise that we need governments around the world, including our own, to take decisive action – and soon.

13 December 2013

⇨ The above information is reprinted with kind permission from Care for the Wild. Please visit www.careforthewild.com for further information.

My manifesto for rewilding the world

Nature swiftly responds when we stop trying to control it. This is our big chance to reverse man's terrible destructive impact.

By George Monbiot

Until modern humans arrived, every continent except Antarctica possessed a megafauna. In the Americas, alongside mastodons, mammoths, four-tusked and spiral-tusked elephants, there was a beaver the size of a black bear: eight feet from nose to tail. There were giant bison weighing two tonnes, which carried horns seven feet across.

The short-faced bear stood 13 feet in its hind socks. One hypothesis maintains that its astonishing size and shocking armoury of teeth and claws are the hallmarks of a specialist scavenger: it specialised in driving giant lions and sabretooth cats off their prey. The Argentine roc (*Argentavis magnificens*) had a wingspan of 26 feet. Sabretooth salmon nine feet long migrated up Pacific coast rivers.

During the previous interglacial period, Britain and Europe contained much of the megafauna we now associate with the tropics: forest elephants, rhinos, hippos, lions and hyenas. The elephants, rhinos and hippos were driven into southern Europe by the ice, then exterminated about 40,000 years ago when modern humans arrived. Lions and hyenas persisted: lions hunted reindeer across the frozen wastes of Britain until 11,000 years ago. The distribution of these animals has little to do with temperature: only where they co-evolved with humans and learned to fear them did they survive.

Most of the deciduous trees in Europe can resprout wherever the trunk is broken. They can survive the extreme punishment – hacking, splitting, trampling – inflicted when a hedge is laid. Understorey trees such as holly, box and yew have much tougher roots and branches than canopy trees, despite carrying less weight. Our trees, in other words, bear strong signs of adaptation to elephants. Blackthorn, which possesses very long spines, seems over-engineered to deter browsing by deer; but not, perhaps, rhinoceros.

All this has been forgotten, even by professional ecologists. Read any paper on elephants and trees in east Africa and it will tell you that many species have adapted to 'hedge' in response to elephant attack. Yet, during a three-day literature search in the Bodleian Library, all I could find on elephant adaptation in Europe was a throwaway sentence in one scientific paper. The elephant in the forest is the elephant in the room: the huge and obvious fact that everyone has overlooked.

Since then much of Europe, especially Britain, has lost most of its mesofauna as well: bison, moose, boar, wolf, bear, lynx, wolverine – even, in most parts, wildcat, beavers and capercaillie. These losses, paradoxically, have often been locked in by conservation policy.

Conservation sites must be maintained in what is called 'favourable condition', which means the condition in which they were found when they were designated. More often than not this is a state of extreme depletion, the merest scraping of what was once a vibrant and dynamic ecosystem. The ecological disasters we call nature reserves are often kept in this depleted state through intense intervention: cutting and burning any trees that return; grazing by domestic animals at greater densities and for longer periods than would ever be found in nature. The conservation ethos is neatly summarised in the forester Ritchie Tassell's sarcastic question, 'how did nature cope before we came along?'

Through rewilding – the mass restoration of ecosystems – I see an opportunity to reverse the destruction of the natural world. Researching my book *Feral*, I came across rewilding programmes in several parts of Europe, including some (such as Trees for Life in Scotland and the Wales Wild Land Foundation) in the UK, which are beginning to show how swiftly nature responds when we stop trying to control it. Rewilding, in my view, should involve reintroducing missing animals and plants, taking down the fences, blocking the drainage ditches, culling a few particularly invasive exotic species but otherwise standing back. It's

about abandoning the biblical doctrine of dominion which has governed our relationship with the natural world.

The only thing preventing a faster rewilding in the EU is public money. Farming is sustained on infertile land (by and large, the uplands) through taxpayers' munificence. Without our help, almost all hill farming would cease immediately. I'm not calling for that, but I do think it's time the farm subsidy system stopped forcing farmers to destroy wildlife. At the moment, to claim their single farm payments, farmers must prevent 'the encroachment of unwanted vegetation on agricultural land'. They don't have to produce anything: they merely have to keep the land in 'agricultural condition', which means bare.

I propose two changes to the subsidy regime. The first is to cap the amount of land for which farmers can claim money at 100 hectares (250 acres). It's outrageous that the biggest farmers harvest millions every year from much poorer

taxpayers, by dint of possessing so much land. A cap would give small farmers an advantage over large. The second is to remove the agricultural condition rule.

The effect of these changes would be to ensure that hill farmers with a powerful attachment to the land and its culture, language and traditions would still farm (and continue to reduce their income by keeping loss-making sheep and cattle). Absentee ranchers who are in it only for the subsidies would find that they were better off taking the money and allowing the land to rewild.

Despite the best efforts of governments, farmers and conservationists, nature is already starting to return. One estimate suggests that two thirds of the previously forested parts of the US have reforested, as farming and logging have retreated, especially from the eastern half of the country.

Another proposes that by 2030, farmers on the European continent (though not in Britain, where no major shift is expected) will vacate around 75 million acres, roughly the size of Poland. While the mesofauna is already beginning to spread back across Europe, land areas of this size could perhaps permit the reintroduction of some of our lost megafauna. Why should Europe not have a Serengeti or two?

Above all, rewilding offers a positive environmentalism. Environmentalists have long known what they are against; now we can explain what we are for. It introduces hope where hope seemed absent. It offers us a chance to replace our silent spring with a raucous summer.

27 May 2013

⇨ The above information is reprinted with kind permission from *The Guardian*. Please visit www.theguardian.com for further information.

Restore large carnivores to save struggling ecosystems

An article from The Conversation.

By William Ripple

We are losing our large carnivores. In ecosystems around the world, the decline of large predators such as lions, bears, dingoes, wolves and otters is changing landscapes, from the tropics to the Arctic. Habitat loss, persecution by humans and loss of prey have combined to inflict great losses on these populations.

In fact more than 75% of the 31 largest carnivore species are declining, and 17 species now occupy less than half their former ranges. Southeast Asia, southern and East Africa, and the Amazon are among areas in which multiple large carnivore species are declining. And with only a few exceptions, large carnivores have already been exterminated from much of the developed world, including areas of Western Europe, and the eastern United States.

Top dogs keep ecosystems in order

Many of these large carnivore species are endangered and some are at risk of extinction, either in specific regions or entirely. Ironically, they are vanishing just as we are learning about their important ecological effects, which is what led us to write a new paper in the journal *Science* to document their role.

From a review of published reports, we singled out seven species that have been studied for their important ecological role and widespread effects, known as trophic cascades. These are the African lion, leopard, Eurasian lynx, cougar, grey wolf, sea otter and dingo.

Based on field research, my Oregon State University co-author Robert Beschta and I documented the impact of cougars and wolves on the regeneration of forest tree stands and riverside vegetation in Yellowstone and other national parks in western North America. Fewer predators, we found, lead to an increase in browsing animals such as deer and elk. More browsing disrupts vegetation, reduces birds and some mammals and changes other parts of the ecosystem. From the actions of the top predator, widespread impacts cascade down the food chain.

Similar effects were found in studies of Eurasian lynx, dingoes, lions and sea otters. For example in Europe, absence of lynx has been closely tied to the abundance of roe deer, red fox and hare. In Australia, the construction of a 3,400-mile dingo-proof fence has enabled scientists to study ecosystems with and without dingoes which are closely related to grey wolves. They found that dingoes control populations of herbivores and exotic red foxes. The suppression of these species by dingoes reduces predation pressure, benefiting plants and smaller native prey.

In some parts of Africa, the decrease of lions and leopards has coincided with a dramatic increase in olive baboons, which threaten crops and livestock. In the waters off southeast Alaska, a decline in sea otters through killer whale predation has led to a rise in sea urchins and loss of kelp beds.

Predators are integral, not expendable

We are now obtaining a deeper appreciation of the impact of large carnivores on ecosystems, a view that can be traced back to the work of landmark ecologist Aldo Leopold. The perception that predators are harmful and deplete fish and wildlife is outdated. Many scientists and wildlife managers now recognise the growing evidence of carnivores' complex role in ecosystems, and their social and economic benefits. Leopold recognised these relationships, but his observations were ignored for decades after his death in 1948.

Human tolerance of these species is the major issue. Most would agree these animals have an intrinsic right to exist, but additionally they provide economic and ecological services that people value. Among

PREDATORS!! BOUNCING BACK!!

the services documented in other studies are carbon sequestration, restoration of riverside ecosystems, biodiversity and disease control. For example, wolves may limit large herbivore populations, thus decreasing browsing on young trees that sequester carbon when they escape browsing and grow taller. Where large carnivore populations have been restored – such as wolves in Yellowstone or Eurasian lynx in Finland – ecosystems appear to be bouncing back.

I am impressed with how resilient the Yellowstone ecosystem is, and while ecosystem restoration isn't happening quickly everywhere in this park, it has started. In some cases where vegetation loss has led to soil erosion, for example, full restoration may not be possible in the near term. What is certain is that ecosystems and the elements of them are highly interconnected. The work at Yellowstone and other places shows how species affect each another through different pathways. It's humbling as a scientist to witness this interconnectedness of nature.

My co-authors and I have called for an international initiative to conserve large carnivores in co-existence with people. This effort could be modelled after a couple of other successful efforts including the Large Carnivore Initiative for Europe, a non-profit scientific group affiliated with the International Union for the Conservation of Nature, and the Global Tiger Initiative which involves all 13 of the tiger-range countries. With more tolerance by humans, we might be able to avoid extinctions. The world would be a scary place without these predators.

9 January 2014

⇨ The above information is reprinted with kind permission from The Conversation Trust (UK). Please visit www.theconversation.com for further information.

Wolf restoration in Yellowstone National Park

Late 1800s-early 1900s

Wolves are routinely killed in Yellowstone National Park.

1926

The last wolf pack in Yellowstone is killed, although reports of single wolves continue.

1974

The grey wolf is listed as endangered; recovery is mandated under the Endangered Species Act.

1975

The long process to restore wolves in Yellowstone begins.

1991

Congress appropriates money for an EIS for wolf recovery.

1994

EIS completed for wolf reintroduction in Yellowstone and central Idaho. More than 160,000 public comments received – the largest number of public comments on any federal proposal at that time.

1995 and 1996

31 grey wolves from western Canada relocated to Yellowstone.

1997

Ten wolves from northwestern Montana relocated to Yellowstone National Park. US District Court judge orders the removal of the reintroduced wolves in Yellowstone, but stays his order, pending appeal. (Decision reversed in 2000.)

1995-2003

Wolves prey on livestock outside Yellowstone much less than expected: 256 sheep, 41 cattle.

2005

Wolf management transfers from the federal government to the states of Idaho and Montana.

2008

Wolf populations in Montana, Idaho and Wyoming removed from the endangered species list, then returned to the list.

2009

The US Fish and Wildlife Service again delisted wolf populations in Montana and Idaho, but not in Wyoming. A legal challenge resulted in the Northern Rocky Mountain wolf population being returned to the federal endangered species list.

2011

Wolf populations were again delisted in Montana and Idaho by action of Congress within the previous year, and the US Fish and Wildlife Service proposed delisting wolves in Wyoming.

2012

Based on a Congressional directive, wolves were delisted in Wyoming and the Northern Rocky Mountain Distinct Population is no longer listed.

⇨ The above information is reprinted with kind permission from the U.S National Park Service. Please visit www.nps.gov.

Penguins in peril

by Pete Haskell

The Equatorial Penguin

Whilst we typically associate penguins with the cold and unforgiving landscape of the South Pole, one species of penguin lives as far away from the poles as you can physically get on Earth. The Galápagos Archipelago is made up of a group of volcanic islands that straddle the equator 1,000km west of Ecuador in the Pacific Ocean. Made famous by Charles Darwin's visit during his voyage on the HMS Beagle in 1835, they are home to thousands of endemic species (those that occur nowhere else in the world). One such species is the Galápagos penguin (*Spheniscus mendiculus*), the most northerly occurring of the 17 species of penguin worldwide.

The key environmental influence that allows Galápagos penguins to

survive at such northerly latitudes is the Humboldt Current. This oceanic current travels up the west coast of South America from Antarctica transporting cold nutrient-rich waters which support schooling fish such as sardines and anchovies; the staple diet of the Galápagos penguin.

In order to cope with the warm air temperatures present in Galápagos, the penguins have had to make a number of adaptations, both physically and behaviourally. Firstly, when compared to their Antarctic cousins, Galápagos penguins have fewer feathers, more areas of bare skin and a higher surface area to volume ratio, all of which help to lose heat. Further heat loss is achieved by swimming in the cool water, panting in a similar way to a dog and extending their flippers out when they are standing on land to allow the cooling sea breeze to circulate around them. Additionally, they nest within lava tubes or deep crevices in the rock where it is naturally shaded to prevent their eggs and chicks from overheating.

But, whilst life on the equator for a penguin is possible, it is by no means easy. Today, the Galápagos penguin is one of the world's rarest penguin species with a population of around 2,000 individuals and it has been listed as endangered by the IUCN for over a decade. With an ever increasing number of threats to this iconic flightless bird, the

conservation management of the remaining colonies is becoming very important. But why are Galápagos penguins so under threat?

Feeling the heat

One of the major threats to penguins is that posed by El Niño, a naturally recurring phenomenon that disrupts the all-important Humboldt Current. This can have dire consequences for Galápagos penguins, as the cold-water schooling fish which they depend so heavily upon move away from the Archipelago during El Niño events. This not only leaves them at risk of starvation, but also means that they breed less frequently because of the extra time and energy required for finding food. It has been observed that no breeding activity takes place at all when water temperatures exceed 25°C, which is not uncommon during El Niño events.

The most dramatic decline in the Galápagos penguin population ever recorded was as a direct result of the 1982–83 El Niño event, which saw a 77% decline in numbers. Whilst El Niño is naturally occurring, global climate change appears to be increasing the frequency and intensity of events, meaning the penguin population has less and less time to recover between episodes.

Other threats to the Galápagos Penguin

In addition to the natural threat presented by El Niño, there are

An indicator species

Because of their reliance on the ocean realm, Galápagos penguin colonies can be used as an indicator of the health of the whole marine environment. Indicator species have been used for decades by researchers to allow them to assess the stability and condition of a particular region. In the instance of Galápagos penguins, consistent monitoring of the population is good for two reasons. Firstly it means that the Galápagos National Park Service can make the most up-to-date management decisions for the protection of the species. Secondly, because of the close connection between food availability and penguin breeding activity, by measuring the latter of these, an assessment can be made about the stocks of schooling fish in the area. This is very valuable information, as many other species also rely on these fish as prey.

significant anthropogenic pressures that Galápagos penguins have to deal with. The most notable of these are the impacts brought by invasive species, a common theme across oceanic archipelagos. One study found that feral cats were the cause of a significant number of deaths within the main penguin breeding colony on Isabela, and introduced rats and fire ants are thought to kill over 50% of penguin eggs every year. A less obvious threat caused by introduced species is the spreading of diseases and parasites. Toxoplasma gondii is a blood parasite which feral cats carry, and it has recently been recorded in Galápagos penguins for the first time. Avian malaria also poses a serious threat. Mosquitoes first arrived in Galápagos in the 1980s and act as a vector for this fatal disease. Fortunately, malaria is yet to be detected in the penguin population, but careful monitoring in the future will be important for safeguarding the species.

Unfortunately, that's not the end of it. Habitat loss, water pollution, oil spills and being caught up in fishing gear all add to the pressures on this species. With such a range of threats both current and potential, monitoring the population is critical to ensuring that the best conservation measures are being effected.

Protecting penguins

The Galápagos Conservation Trust is the only UK charity set up solely to support projects in Galápagos. Working in collaboration with the Charles Darwin Foundation and Galápagos National Park, both of which are based on the Islands, they support the essential monitoring and research of the Galápagos penguin population each year. This helps to ensure that the best conservation measures are in place and acts to secure a brighter future for the penguins of Galápagos.

1 April 2014

⇨ The above information is reprinted with kind permission from Pete Haskell. Please visit www.savegalapagos.org and www.discoveringgalapagos. org.uk for further information.

© Pete Haskell, 2014

Giant tortoises show rewilding can work

Exotic species can be used to restore important functions in ecosystems that were lost following the extinction of key species, according to a new study of giant tortoises on a small island in the Indian Ocean. The study was carried out by an international team of researchers led by the University of Bristol.

'Rewilding with taxon substitutes', the intentional introduction of exotic species to fulfil key functions in ecosystems following the loss of recently extinct species, is highly controversial, partly due to a lack of rigorous scientific studies.

In a paper published today in *Current Biology*, Christine Griffiths of Bristol's School of Biological Sciences and colleagues present the first empirical evidence that rewilding can work.

Exotic giant Aldabra tortoises, *Aldabrachelys gigantea*, were introduced to Ile aux Aigrettes, a 25-hectare island off Mauritius, in 2000 to disperse the slow-growing ebony *Diospyros egrettarum* (Ebenaceae), which once covered the island, but today is critically endangered following intensive logging for firewood that lasted until the early 1980s.

To highlight the extent to which the ebony forest had been decimated, the researchers surveyed and mapped all ebony trees in an island-wide survey in 2007 and located a total of 3,518 adult trees. However, large tracts of the island remained denuded of ebony, particularly in the northern and eastern coastal areas nearest to the mainland where logging was most intense.

There had been no regeneration in these areas even though logging ceased 30 years ago because, with the extinction of the island's native giant tortoises, there were no large fruit-eating animals left to disperse the seeds of these critically-endangered trees.

The introduced Aldabra tortoises not only ingested the large fruits and dispersed large numbers of ebony seeds, but the process of passing through a tortoise's gut also improved seed germination, leading to the widespread, successful establishment of new ebony seedlings in the heavily logged parts of the island.

> **'Exotic species can be used to restore important functions in ecosystems that were lost following the extinction of key species'**

Christine Griffiths said: 'Our results demonstrate that the introduction of these effective seed dispersers is aiding the recovery of this critically endangered tree whose seeds were previously seed-dispersal limited. Reversible rewilding experiments such as ours are necessary to investigate whether extinct interactions can be restored.'

Professor Stephen Harris, co-author of the study, said: 'Ecological restoration projects generally involve the plant community, as more often the animal components are extinct. There is, however, increasing evidence that restoration ecologists should be most concerned with the decline of species interactions, rather than species extinctions per se. Species interactions structure ecological communities, and provide essential ecosystem processes and functions such as pollination, seed dispersal and browsing, that are necessary for the self-regulation and persistence of a community.'

21 April 2011

⇨ The above information is reprinted with kind permission from the University of Bristol. Please visit www.bristol.ac.uk for further information.

© University of Bristol

Key facts

- There are 18 species of bat in Britain and all of them are endangered. (page 1)

- Globally, there are around 320 Amur tigers in the wild. This has increased from just 20 in the 1930s. (page 1)

- Morocco is home to 95% of the truly wild colonies of the ibis. (page 1)

- Around 1.5 million species of animal have been named and described by scientists. (page 2)

- Dinosaurs are the most well-known example of natural extinction. They appeared on Earth about 200 million years ago and dominated both land and sea for almost 100 million years. (page 2)

- There have been at least five episodes of mass extinctions in the past, during which anywhere from 60% to 95% of existing species became extinct. (page 4)

- 99% of all species that have ever existed are now extinct. (page 4)

- 875 species have been recorded as declining to extinction between 1500 and 2009. (page 4)

- The *ICUN Red List of Threatened Species* notes that 36% of the 47,677 species assessed are threatened with extinction. This represents 21% of mammals, 30% of amphibians, 12% of birds, 28% of reptiles, 37% of freshwater fishes, 70% of plants and 35% of invertebrates. (page 5)

- More than three quarters of large carnivores are in decline, and 17 species occupy less than half of their historical distributions. (page 6)

- Just 1,000 grey long-eared bats remain in the UK and numbers are declining. (page 7)

- Between 25,000 and 40,000 elephants are likely to be killed in 2013 and South Africa is projected to lose between 900 and 1,000 rhinoceroses to poachers by Christmas 2013. (page 9)

- As few as 400 tigers are thought to remain in the rainforests of Sumatra. (page 12)

- 10% of all remaining forested tiger habitat remained at risk of clearance in pulp and oil palm concessions in 2011. (page 12)

- China's wild tiger population currently stands at just 30 tigers. (page 14)

- The findings published in the report *Killing with Keystrokes: An Investigation of the Illegal Wildlife Trade on the World Wide Web (2008),* recorded a staggering 7,122 online auctions, advertisements and classifieds, with an advertised value of $3.87 million. (page 17)

- The International Fund for Animal Welfare report *Killing with Keystrokes 2.0* found that the total advertised value of online ivory ads in the UK was 11,539.80 EUR (approximately £9,505.14). (page 20)

- By the end of September 2013, a record 704 rhinos had been killed by poachers in South Africa. (page 21)

- Cases of the illegal persecution of British birds is continuing to rise, a report from the RSPB showed that there were 208 reports of the shooting and destruction of birds of prey in 2012. (page 21)

- A recent 2013 estimate valued the illegal poaching trade in Africa as being worth $17 billion dollars a year and growing. (page 23)

- Animal rights groups estimate that poachers in Africa kill between 25,000 and 35,000 elephants annually – meaning about 104 die every day. (page 23)

- In February 2014, conservationists at Sabah in Malaysia celebrated a breakthrough sentence which saw two palm oil planation workers jailed for 2 years for killing an orangutan. (page 26)

- Hunters have been known to pay up to US$125,000 to shoot a male lion. (page 31)

Conservation

Safeguarding biodiversity; attempting to protect endangered species and their habitats from destruction.

Deforestation

The clearance of large areas of forest to obtain wood or land for cattle grazing.

Ecosystem

A system maintained by the interaction between different biological organisms within their physical environment, each one of which is important for the ecosystem to continue to function efficiently.

Endangered

A species which is at risk of becoming extinct.

Endemic

Native or restricted to a particular place.

Extinct

If a species has become extinct, there are no surviving members of that species: it has died out completely.

Habitat

An area which supports certain conditions, allowing various species native to that area to live and thrive. When a species' 'natural habitat' is mentioned, this refers to the area it would usually occupy in the wild.

ICUN Red List of Threatened Species

The most commonly-used measure of how endangered a species has become is the IUCN Red List, which classifies endangered species as either Critically Endangered (CR), meaning that a species faces extremely high risk of extinction in the near future; Endangered (EN), meaning that a species faces a very high risk of extinction in the near future and Vulnerable (VU), meaning that a species is likely to become Endangered unless the circumstances threatening its survival and reproduction improve.

Invertebrate

Animal without a backbone.

Natural extinction

If a species becomes extinct due to natural causes (as opposed to human causes such as poaching).

Palm oil

Palm oil is the world's most popular vegetable oil. It is used in many products, including pizza, make-up and soap. Oil palm plantations are making a significant contribution to deforestation and ecosystem destruction.

Rewilding

Reintroducing a species that previously inhabited an natural area.

Species

A specific type of living organism.

Wildlife trade

The sale of wild animals, increasingly achieved through use of the Internet to advertise and promote auctions.

Assignments

Brainstorm

⇨ In small groups, brainstorm to find out what you know about endangered and extinct species. Consider the following points:

- What is extinction?

- What do we mean when we say that a species is 'endangered'?

- Can you think of any endangered species?

- What do you know about wildlife conservation?

- What causes species to become endangered or extinct?

Research

⇨ Research a wildlife conservation project in the UK and share your findings with the rest of your class.

⇨ Why did the dinosaurs become extinct? Do some research and write some notes on your findings.

⇨ Choose one of the endangered animals from the article on page one and research it further. Make some notes and tell your class what you found out. Include anything you found particularly interesting about your chosen species.

⇨ Do some research and find out more about palm oil. Which household products use palm oil? Write some notes on your findings and discuss with the rest of your class.

⇨ Over the course of a week, make notes about news stories about endangered and extinct species. At the end of the week, report back to your class with a news roundup.

⇨ Do some research and find out more about the ivory trade. Make some notes and feedback to your class.

Oral

⇨ Is it important to save animals from extinction? Discuss this question in pairs and feed back to the rest of your class.

⇨ As a class, stage a debate around the question 'Do elephants deserve foreign aid?' Half of the class should argue *yes* and the other half should argue *no*.

⇨ In pairs, discuss whether you think scientists should be allowed to bring extinct animals back to life. Summarise your arguments in favour and against, and feedback to the rest of your class.

⇨ Which animal would you be most sad to lose if it became extinct? Discuss in pairs.

Design

⇨ In pairs, imagine that you are setting up a charity that will raise awareness of, and work towards, the conservation of an endangered UK species. Choose your species, think of a name for your charity, design a logo, and then make a PowerPoint presentation explaining why your species is important and what your charity will do to protect it. Your presentation should last for no more than ten minutes.

⇨ Design a leaflet that explains the concept behind 'rewilding'.

⇨ Design a campaign that will raise awareness of online wildlife trafficking. You could choose a radio ad, television ad or a series of posters.

⇨ Choose an article in this book and create your own illustration to accompany it.

Reading/Writing

⇨ If you could bring an endangered species back to life, what would it be and why? Write a blog post exploring your ideas.

⇨ Do you think that game reserves should allow people to pay to hunt large animals, like lions, if they then use that money towards conservation? Use the articles in this book to help you form an opinion, do some further research if necessary, and write an essay of no more than 1,000 words as an answer to the question.

⇨ Read the article 'We need to abolish all zoos'... on page 32 and write a letter to the author explaining whether you agree or disagree with his point of view.

⇨ Write a summary, no more than two sides of A4, exploring why some species become endangered.

⇨ Watch *Attenborough's Ark: A Natural World Special* and write a review, considering whether you agree with David Attenborough's 'top ten' endangered species.

⇨ Read *Endangered animals of the world* on pages one to three and write a summary for your school newspaper.

Acknowledgements

The publisher is grateful for permission to reproduce the material in this book. While every care has been taken to trace and acknowledge copyright, the publisher tenders its apology for any accidental infringement or where copyright has proved untraceable. The publisher would be pleased to come to a suitable arrangement in any such case with the rightful owner.

Images

Cover, pages iii and 13: iStock, page 1 (top left) © Gilles San Martin, page 1 (bottom left) © Roman Stanek, page 1 (top right) © Damien du Toit, page 1 (bottom right) © Martin Pettitt, page 4: MorgueFile, page 8 © Jan Arendtsz, page 17: iStock, page 18 © Dan Marsh, page 24 © Cara Acred, page 26 © Colin Knowles, pages 30 and 31 © Luke Hunter/Panthera, page 32: iStock, page 34: MorgueFile, page 35 © Steve Cole, page 38 © Sabine Van Der Meulen.

Illustrations

Don Hatcher: pages 5 and 23. Simon Kneebone: pages 3 and 36. Angelo Madrid: pages 16 and 28.

Additional acknowledgements

Editorial on behalf of Independence Educational Publishers by Cara Acred.

With thanks to the Independence team: Mary Chapman, Sandra Dennis, Christina Hughes, Jackie Staines and Jan Sunderland.

Cara Acred

Cambridge

May 2014